To a Different Drum

To a Different Drum
The Story of Henry David Thoreau

by Charles Norman
Author of *The Playmaker of Avon*

Pictures by Margaret Bloy Graham

HARPER & ROW, PUBLISHERS

New York, Evanston, and London

TO A DIFFERENT DRUM

Copyright, 1954, by Charles Norman

Printed in the United States of America

Library of Congress catalog card number: 54-8977

To Michael and
Samuel Adams McCleery

Foreword

WHO has not wanted to build a hut in the woods? Henry Thoreau built one with his own hands and lived in it for two years and two months. It was the great experience of his life, and from it came the masterpiece called *Walden*.

Thoreau believed that men spent too much of their time acquiring things they did not need; his sojourn by Walden Pond demonstrated how little he, for one, needed to support life agreeably. "I went to the woods," he wrote, "because I wished to live deliberately, to front only the essential facts of life, and see if I could not learn what it had to teach, and not, when I came to die, discover that I had not lived."

With his great gifts, Thoreau could have been successful in almost any endeavor where brains and character count. But, as Emerson said of him, "he chose to be rich by making his wants few, and supplying them himself." It left him all the time he needed for the observation of Nature, which was his passion. He was, as he said of himself, "self-appointed inspector of snow storms and rain storms," one moreover who "frequently tramped eight or ten miles through the deepest snow to keep an appointment with a beech tree, or a yellow birch, or an old acquaintance among the pines."

A man so completely at home in the outdoors was bound to be less at his ease in polite society. He said some sharp things—which were none the less sharp for being true—and it was sometimes awkward to have him around. He hated shams and injustice; he scorned joiners, hypocrites and bores. It is not surprising that he preferred the company of children to that of their elders, and was "always ready to lead a huckleberry party." But in upholding his own right to be the kind of individual he was, he spoke for all: "If a man does not keep pace with his companions, perhaps it is because he hears a different drummer. Let him step to the music which he hears, however measured or far away."

Thoreau died in 1862. Years later, the great naturalist John Burroughs wrote of him: "He improves with age—in fact requires age to take off a little of his asperity, and fully ripen him. The world likes a good hater and refuser almost as well as it likes a good lover and acceptor—only it likes him a little farther off."

But instead of becoming farther off with the passage of time, Thoreau seems to come closer. It is even tempting to quote his words about John Brown and apply them to himself, for time has made them applicable: "Think of him—of his rare qualities!— such a man as it takes ages to make, and ages to understand; no mock hero, nor the representative of any party." Indeed, his life is so bound up with his writing, and his writing is so much a part of his life, that I have quoted generously. What else was there to do with a man who wrote in his journal: "I had no idea that there was so much going on in Heywood's meadow"?

I am glad of this opportunity of thanking my friend Henry Christman for placing his collection of Thoreau material at my disposal, a gesture which enormously lightened my task, and a fit one for the son of the poet and naturalist, W. W. Christman, who was a friend of John Burroughs.

C. N.

Contents

1. The Building of the Hut   1

2. Thoreau and His Family   13

3. The Schoolmaster Who Didn't Flog   22

4. The River Voyage   26

5. The River Voyage (Concluded)   32

6. In Emerson's House   44

7. *Walden*   53

8. Thoreau and the Fugitive Slave   71

9. With Emerson's Children   76

10. In the Public Eye   83

11. Thoreau Meets Walt Whitman   92

12. The Speech in the Vestry   98

13. The Death of Thoreau   107

14. Epilogue   110

To a Different Drum

Chapter One

The Building of the Hut

O N A March day in 1845, a man carrying an **axe**
left the town of Concord, Massachusetts, walking
south. His pace was long, uniform, unfaltering. Like
an Indian's, some of his townsmen thought as they saw
him going off on another of his rambles in the woods.
As a matter of fact, though few knew it, his mind
dwelled continually on the Indians who had once hunted
there. Indians—and the great herds of moose that had
ranged southward from Canada, and now ranged no
more. His eyes were quick to detect the circles in the
sand where the red man's tents had stood along the two
rivers that held the township in embrace; and there was
something uncanny about the ease with which he could
pick up arrowheads wherever he went. No wonder children liked to go on walks with him; and, occasionally,
a grownup as well.

Only five feet seven inches tall, his sturdy build hinted

at great powers of endurance. His complexion was that of a man who had lived much in the open air—indeed, his face had the rugged and ruddy look of an Egyptian statue. His nose, though aquiline, was somewhat too large to be handsome—it even drooped a bit. His mouth, however, was finely shaped and capable of pleasant speech; it was also capable, as some had learned to their chagrin, of uttering tart, terse truths, or of being shut firmly in scorn. But it was his eyes that were truly remarkable: gray-blue in color, and of a piercing keenness. They not only saw where arrowheads lay, but the slightest stirring of bush or bough, the tobogganing of a leaf, the delicate etching of tracks in the snow; and they seemed made as well to pierce through sham and pretense. He was a disconcerting neighbor at times.

The clothes he had on were plain and strong—he cared nothing about them except that they should serve him well, the longer the better. His cowhide shoes were sturdy, and not only unpolished but scuffed. He looked like a farmer; but a second glance would suffice to reveal that he was no ordinary one. A flute stuck out of a pocket. Even among the highly individualistic Yankees of the region a man carrying both an axe and a flute was a little unusual.

His name was Henry David Thoreau. He had been christened David Henry, but he preferred it the other way around. His destination was the woods above

Walden Pond, a mile and a half from Concord, where he planned to build a hut—and to live in it. He had only a few dollars to his name; of property he had none. He preferred it that way. "I love a broad margin to my life," he said. Weren't the woods, fields, sky and water, his for the asking?

"For many years," he was to write, "I was self-appointed inspector of snow storms and rain storms, and did my duty faithfully; surveyor, if not of highways, then of forest paths and all across-lot routes, keeping them open, and ravines bridged and passable at all seasons."

It was the truth. Hardly a day had passed in all his twenty-eight years that had not found him a strenuous walker in the open air. But never in his unceasing explorations of the countryside around Concord had Thoreau walked with jauntier step. It was as though he walked to a merry tune of the flute which he carried and could play so well.

On that late March day in 1845 the ice in Walden Pond had not yet melted, and the wind on the hillside in the pine woods where he planned to build nipped shrewdly. Snow fell in brief, slight flurries. Undeterred, he took off his round farmer's hat, revealing light brown hair parted on one side, but not too carefully combed. With a well-aimed blow of his axe he struck near the base of a tall, arrowy white pine. A second blow followed, then another, and another, until the scented chips were flying. Warming to his work, he warmed himself in the process. Soon, several trees lay in their green-clad lengths on the hard ground.

From time to time he looked down at the pond that he loved. It was half a mile long, and a mile and three-quarters in circumference. The spring thaw was at hand, and his keen glance detected some open spaces in the ice. He continued chopping. In pauses he could hear the first birds, back from their winter sojourns in the south. From branches where patches of snow still clung they sang that spring had come, and at last, before ceasing work for the day, he snatched the flute from his pocket and piped a reply to their brave notes. He piped like the expert he was, and the music of his flute rang out high, sweet, and melodious in the pine woods.

The next day he returned to his labors. Lopping the branches from the pines that he had felled, he cut and hewed timber, studs, and rafters for his hut. His axe head came off. He cut a green hickory for a wedge, drove it in with a stone, then descended to the shore, where he placed the axe in a pond-hole to soak and swell the wood. As he did so, a striped snake slithered into the water and lay there motionless. Letting the axe soak, Thoreau watched the snake, fascinated; and the snake, apparently, watched him from the bottom of the pond. Thoreau wondered if it had yet come out of its torpid

state from which it had been roused by spring, for it
stayed a full quarter of an hour under water.

"It appeared to me," he commented afterwards, "that
for a like reason men remain in their present low and
primitive condition; but if they should feel the influence
of the spring of springs arousing them, they would of
necessity rise to a higher and more ethereal life."

Thus he philosophized and returned to his work.

The days passed. On April 1 it rained; the ice began
to melt. A wild goose cackled and groped its way above
the mist rising from the pond. It sounded to Thoreau
"like the spirit of the fog." He liked it none the less
for that.

Sitting amid the green pine boughs which he had
lopped off with his axe, he ate his midday meal of bread
and butter and read the newspaper in which it had been
wrapped. His hands were sticky with pine pitch, and
gave the bread a piney flavor. He enjoyed his bread the
more.

Soon the frame for his hut was ready for raising
and boarding. Thoreau put his axe down and set out.

Not far from the site he had chosen stood the home
of James Collins, an Irishman who had worked on the
Fitchburg Railroad, which ran past the woods above
Walden Pond. Collins was moving on. He had been
living in a shanty with a peaked cottage roof and
boarded walls. There was no doorsill; under the door-

board was a passage for hens. As Thoreau entered the
shanty, the hens flew inside and a cat flew out the
window.

It was dark inside. Mrs. Collins lit a lamp. Thoreau
was now able to get a view of the interior. The floor
was mostly dirt, with here and there a board. The
furniture consisted of a stove, a bed, a mirror in a gilt
frame, and a coffee mill.

A brief discussion, and Thoreau and Mr. Collins
shook hands on their bargain, *viz.*—Henry handed over
$4.25 for the shanty, minus its furniture, the tenants
to vacate by five the next morning, "selling to nobody
else meanwhile." Thoreau was to take possession at
six.

The next morning, Thoreau passed the Irishman and
his family—there was also an infant—on the road. They
were carrying everything with them, including the
hens. The cat had been left behind. Thoreau afterwards
learned it had taken to the woods, become wild, and had
stepped into a trap for woodchucks.

He dismantled the shanty the same morning. Using
a cart, he carried the boards to the site of his hut. Each
cartload of boards was laid out on the grass to bleach
and warp back again in the sun, and as he went to
and fro, a wood thrush whistled cheerily from a neigh-
boring tree. The boards from the shanty were not
enough, and he purchased some additional ones.

Down through sumach and blackberry roots, where a woodchuck had once dug his burrow, Henry dug his cellar. It was six feet square and seven feet deep. He had come to a fine sand, and knew that potatoes would not freeze there in the severest winter. He stopped digging.

Early in May he raised the frame of his hut. In this he was helped by several Concord friends—"rather to improve so good an occasion for neighborliness than from any necessity," he afterwards recorded. At the far end of the single room he laid the foundation for a chimney, with stones brought from the shore up the hill in his arms. Roofing and boarding followed. The boards were feather-edged and made to lap each other, so that the hut was snug and proof against wind and rain.

The hut was ten feet wide by fifteen long, with eight-feet posts. There was a large window on either side, a garret and a closet, two trap doors, and a door which faced downhill towards the pond. Not counting the labor of his hands, it had cost exactly the following, as itemized by himself:

Boards	$8.03½
Refuse shingles for roof and sides	4.00
Laths	1.25

Two second-hand windows
    with glass 2.43
One thousand old brick 4.00
Two casks of lime 2.40
Hair 0.31
Mantle-tree iron 0.15
Nails 3.90
Hinges and screws 0.14
Latch 0.10
Chalk....................   0.01
Transportation 1.40
    In all $28.12½

Next to some of these items he made certain comments. "That was high," he wrote after the $2.40 for the casks of lime. "More than I needed," he put down after the thirty-one cents worth of hair. After "Transportation," he wrote: "I carried a good part on my back." From the materials that were left over he built a woodshed behind the hut.

He had also constructed part of the furniture. The furniture consisted of a bed, a table, a desk, three chairs, a looking glass—it was only three inches in diameter—a pair of tongs and andirons, a kettle, a skillet, a frying pan, a dipper and a washbowl. His utensils were: two knives and forks, but only one spoon; three plates and one cup. He had also a jug for oil, a jug for molasses, and a japanned lamp. Three chairs! As he himself remarked: "None is so poor that he need sit on a pumpkin."

In the light and sandy soil near the hut he planted two and a half acres of beans, potatoes, corn, peas, and turnips. A farmer, stopping by, told him: "You cannot live on vegetable food solely, for it furnishes nothing to make bones with." Thoreau smiled over the reflection that the farmer, eating meat every day "to supply his system with the raw material of bones," had to walk behind his oxen which, with their vegetable-formed bones, carried him and his plow along.

His house was now ready to receive him. Perhaps it was significant that he dawdled until July 4—Independence Day—before moving in. Monarch of all he surveyed, as he looked out at the woods and the water of Walden Pond his hand went to his flute, the flute to his lips, and he piped a serenade to Nature, solitude, and independence. From bush and branch, bright eyes and little ears watched and listened. From that time on, he was regularly serenaded in turn. On mornings when the mist stole from the pond, and the grass was wet with dew, the birds sang out to him from their dim-lit auditorium in the leaves. By day the sweet notes of the wood thrush—"Ee-o-lay, ee-o-lay"—came to him; by night the whippoorwill, close at hand, and the owl afar, led the unending orchestration of the woods.

"An abode without birds is like a meat without seasoning."

He found himself suddenly neighbor to the birds—not by having imprisoned any, but by caging himself near them.

"I intend," he wrote in his journal, "to build me a house which will surpass any on the main street in Concord in grandeur and luxury, as soon as it pleases me as much and will cost me no more than my present one."

Such was the hermit of Walden Pond. He could breathe, he could stretch, and he could utter his thoughts, if not to another human being, at least—without interruption—to his journal. Glancing proudly around at his handiwork, he contrasted his hut with the room he had inhabited at Harvard. His hut had cost him $28.12½, and he knew that it would last for some time to come.

"I will endeavor to speak a good word for the truth," he wrote. "At Cambridge College the mere rent of a student's room, which is only a little larger than my own, is thirty dollars each year, though the corporation had the advantage of building thirty-two side by side and under one roof, and the occupant suffers the inconvenience of many and noisy neighbors, and perhaps a residence in the fourth story."

At Walden, he was on the ground floor—one step and he was on the ground itself, with a lake—so to speak—for a yard. He would not have exchanged it for a king's palace.

He began to hoe his bean field. A farmer—perhaps the same one who had told him that he could not live "on vegetable food solely"—remarked that the soil was "good for nothing but to raise cheeping squirrels on." But Thoreau got twelve bushels of beans, eighteen bushels of potatoes, and some peas and sweet corn in addition. The yellow corn and turnips "were too late to come to anything." He sold what he couldn't use himself for $23.44.

He had spent $14.72½ for implements, seed, and the hire of a team and a man for plowing. But he had held the plow himself. In the plowing he got several cords of stumps which, together with the dead wood behind his house and the driftwood from the pond, gave him a supply of fuel. He built the chimney in the fall. Until then, he cooked outdoors.

"I desire to speak impartially on this point," he exulted, "and as one not interested in the success or failure of the present economical and social arrangements. I was more independent than any farmer in Concord, for I was not anchored to a house or farm, but could follow the bent of my genius, which is a very crooked one, every moment. Besides being better off than they already, if my house had been burned or my crops had failed, I should have been nearly as well off as before."

He returned the axe he had borrowed.

"The owner of the axe, as he released his hold on it, said that it was the apple of his eye," Thoreau wrote; "but I returned it sharper than I received it."

Chapter Two

Thoreau and His Family

THE town that Henry Thoreau had left behind for the woods of Walden was renowned in the history of the young Republic. There, on the morning of April 19, 1775, was fired the shot heard round the world. Immortal now in bronze, the Minute Man still watches over Concord, one hand on his plow, the other grasping a musket. Under his gaze, in the field where they fell, British soldiers lie buried together.

Beyond the markers and monuments to American liberty, in the pleasant, tree-lined streets, stand the stately homes of famous citizens. Off the road that leads to Lexington, where the embattled farmers also faced the British, is Orchard House, home of Louisa May Alcott, who has described it in *Little Women*. It was her father, Bronson Alcott, who had lent Thoreau the axe used at Walden Pond. Behind a prim white picket fence is the home of Ralph Waldo Emerson,

who owned the land on which Thoreau built his hut. Framed by towering elms is the Old Manse, where Nathaniel Hawthorne lived and wrote, and whose garden Thoreau had put in order for the newcomer and his bride.

Fields and meadows surround the town, and winding past them flow, as they flowed in Indian days, the Concord and Sudbury rivers, with Walden Pond to the south. Thoreau first saw Walden Pond while he was still a child. He had never forgotten it. A month after he went to live there, he wrote in his journal: "When I was five years old, I was brought from Boston to this pond away in the country—which was then but another name for the extended world. . . . That woodland vision for a long time made the drapery of my dreams."

He had been born in Concord—indeed, of the famous trio of American worthies dwelling in that famous town, Emerson, Hawthorne, and Thoreau, he alone had been born there. The date was July 12, 1817. Shortly after his birth his family moved, but they returned to Concord several years later.

The house he was born in stood on the Virginia Road, just outside Concord. It was a gray house, unpainted for a long time, unfenced, with a brook in front, and a view of the Walden woods beyond. The Thoreau family lived in a kind of genteel poverty; later, their fortunes mended somewhat.

Henry's father, John Thoreau, was the son of a Protestant French emigrant from the Isle of Jersey, one of the Channel Islands. His mother was Cynthia Dunbar, who had been born in Keene, New Hampshire, the daughter of a Congregational minister. Henry Thoreau grew up speaking with a burr, which he supposed to be French, but which more likely came from his Scotch mother and grandmother. When the subject of family histories came up—as it always does in small communities—he liked to imagine that his family name was originally Scandinavian, and that it was the same as a mythical hero's, "Thorer, the Dog-footed." He did not press the point.

His father had been an unsuccessful storekeeper, first in Concord, then in nearby Chelmsford. Had the Thoreau family stayed in Chelmsford another year, Henry might have attended school under the man who was to be his friend in later life, for Emerson taught there. But failure drove Henry's father to fresh fields, this time to Boston, where the 1822 Directory lists him as a schoolmaster.

In 1823 the family returned to Concord. There John Thoreau went into the manufacture of lead pencils. His pencils rivaled the European ones for quality; later, when Henry put his mind and hands into the business, the pencils became even better.

John Thoreau was a quiet man, cautious and secre-

tive, and more of a listener than a talker, which may
have been the result of his shopkeeping experiences.
His handwriting was beautiful. His mind was stored
with Concord lore, and he was reputed to know more
about that town's worthies and unworthies than any
other resident. Mrs. Thoreau, however, was more of
a talker than a listener. She talked in a monologue,
pell-mell. She was a great gossip, and villagers, seeing
her rushing down the street with her yellow bonnet
ribbons fluttering behind her, wondered what choice
morsel she was bearing. Nevertheless, she was a good
housekeeper. One visitor said her bread, both the
brown and the white, was the best he ever tasted. She
also made delectable pies. When she was not talking or
cooking, she read, and like her husband, she was a
nature lover. The Thoreaus often took their children
on nature walks, and it was on one of these that Henry
first saw Walden Pond.

Henry grew up with a serious, almost grave expression, a dreamer by the window between the Bible and
the wax flowers under glass. He disliked games, and
made himself scarce when there was company. If he
could not leave the house, he got as far away as he
could, sitting by a window to watch birds. At the age
of ten he wrote an essay entitled "The Seasons." Already the outdoors was in his blood. It was not only high
hawks circling in the sky, the far-off bark of the fox,

the droll stance of the vigilant woodchuck—nose in the wind and pointed ears tense with listening—that brought ecstasy to the young wanderer in the fields and woods. About once a year a canal boat came up the Concord River, stealing mysteriously through the meadows and past the village, and he ran to the riverside to see it pass, marveling at its great size, its buoyancy, and pondering the strange fact that the men who worked on it actually *slept* on board.

With his brother John he sometimes shouldered a gun and went into the woods to hunt. Once they went night fishing, with homemade spears and an old tin pan with a hole in the bottom in which they built a fire by whose light they hoped to attract fish. After they had speared a few, the crate in which the pan was encased caught fire, and down it plunged with a loud sizzling sound.

In the family there were also two sisters—Helen, the oldest, cut in the mold of a spinster from the start, but an intellectual type; and Sophia, the youngest, who painted, but not well, and loved flowers, which she brought into the house in profusion. In addition, there were boarders, some of them Mrs. Thoreau's kin, so that the Thoreau children grew up with the usual assortment of eccentric uncles and aunts around. Henry's Uncle Charles, for example, could swallow knives and make things disappear. Henry learned his tricks.

At sixteen Henry Thoreau entered Harvard on a

scholarship. He had prepared for the university at Concord Academy. One look from President Quincy of Harvard was enough to reveal that Thoreau was bright; but he certainly was not prepossessing. His grave expression, which had won him the nickname of "The Judge"; his homespun clothes, hardly in repair; his unkempt mane of hair; but most of all, his independent air, made the president of Harvard look upon him with an unsympathetic eye.

"You have barely got in," he told the youth from Concord.

If President Quincy had tried to rattle him, Thoreau succeeded in rattling President Quincy and some of the professors as well. In an essay he wrote at Harvard occur two sentences which must have rung strangely amid those academic bowers in the shadow of Boston:

"Our Indian is more of a man than the inhabitant of a city."

"Learning is Art's creature, but it is not essential to the perfect man; it cannot educate."

When later his friend Emerson remarked that at Harvard they taught all the branches of learning, Thoreau replied: "Yes, indeed, all the branches and none of the roots."

Thoreau read omnivorously, chiefly, it would appear, the philosophies of India and the old English poets, for

whom he cherished a love all his life. Before he left
Harvard he was able to read Latin and Greek for his
own pleasure, had learned French, and had got a smat-
tering of Spanish and Italian. He learned about German
literature from Professor Henry Wadsworth Longfellow, just back from Europe. Longfellow was a dandy,
and wore light kid gloves and wine-colored waistcoats.
Thoreau wore a green homespun coat to chapel, although black was required. He could not afford another,
and in any case, clothes were the least of his preoccu-
pations.

How did Thoreau look to his classmates at this
time? One of them has told how his "prominent, gray-
blue eyes seemed to rove down the path, just in advance
of his feet, as his grave Indian stride carried him down
to University Hall. This down-looking habit was Chau-
cer's also, who walked as if a great deal of surmising
went on between the earth and him."

He rattled President Quincy and others in his audience with his Commencement speech on August 16,
1837. The other members of the graduating class,
which was a small one, also spoke, but are forgotten.
Thoreau declared, echoing Emerson, though perhaps
unconsciously:

"This curious world which we inhabit is more won-
derful than it is convenient; more beautiful than it is

useful; it is more to be admired and enjoyed than used. The order of things should be somewhat reversed; the seventh should be man's day of toil, wherein to earn his living by the sweat of his brow; and the other six his Sabbath of the affections and the soul—in which to range this widespread garden, and drink in the soft influences and sublime revelations of Nature."

President and faculty were probably glad to see the last of him. He was graduated with a B.A. In order to receive the actual diploma he had to pay a dollar for it. He passed it up. To Emerson he said: "Let every sheep keep but his own skin, I say." For the class record he afterwards wrote:

"Though bodily I have been a member of Harvard University, heart and soul I have been far away among the scenes of my boyhood. Those hours that should have been devoted to study, have been spent in scouring the woods and exploring the lakes and streams of my native village."

Chapter Three

The Schoolmaster Who Didn't Flog

WHEN Henry returned home from Harvard, he fled from his family and the boarders to a garret room with yellow walls. There, with his books and papers—for he had already begun to write—he pondered his future employment. He fled outdoors, and pondered some more. Even a treasure-cache of arrowheads, rare birds and rarer flowers of the woods, could not for long drive the persistent thought away. He was twenty—he had to find a job.

Teaching naturally suggested itself. But even there his original bent of mind came into opposition with society. His ideas about the education of the young were somewhat advanced. He did not, for example, believe in corporal punishment—an unusual, not to say alarming and revolutionary notion in 1837. He also looked on young people as individuals:

"I could make education a pleasant thing both to the teacher and the scholar. This discipline which we allow to be the end of life, should not be one thing in the schoolroom, and another in the street. We should seek to be fellow students with the pupil, and we should learn of, as well as with him, if we would be most helpful to him. . . . I have ever been disposed to regard the cowhide as a non-conductor."

He got a job teaching in the Concord elementary school. Two weeks later a deacon who was a member of the school board walked in. The deacon was indignant. What—no flogging?

"You must flog and use the ferule," he exclaimed, "or the school will spoil."

Here was a dilemma. Thoreau solved it dramatically. Was it flogging and feruling the school board wanted? Why, then, my masters, here—you—and you—and you —and you—and you—and you. He feruled six pupils, innocent and guilty, sheep and goats; and amid their caterwauling resigned and walked out.

He was once again without a job.

Over the familiar across-lots route he went, past meadow and grove towards the Cambridge Turnpike. The black-coated deacon flapped like a scarecrow in the garden of his thoughts. He tried to be serious, but his laughter bubbled over, and he shared his mirth with the astonished birds. He came at last to Emerson's house behind its white picket fence. For a moment he was overcome by shyness; then he knocked. The philosopher's welcome could not have been warmer, and Henry was soon talking at his ease in Emerson's study. Emerson afterwards wrote in his journal (everybody—everybody, that is, who could write—kept one): "My good Henry Thoreau made this else solitary afternoon sunny with his simplicity and clear perception. How comic is simplicity in this double-dealing, quacking world. Everything that boy says makes merry with society, though nothing can be graver than his meaning."

Their talk had its practical side. As a result, in the Parkman House at the corner of Main Street and Sudbury Road, Henry opened a school with his brother John. There was no interference with their method. "It was a peculiar school," one of the students afterwards recalled; "there was never a boy flogged or threatened, yet I never saw so absolutely military discipline. How it was done I scarcely know. Even the incorrigible were brought into line." After morning prayers, one of the brothers gave a little talk. Henry's talks were chiefly on Nature; but once he gave a lecture on profanity. According to another student, it went something like this:

"Boys, if you went to talk business with a man, and he persisted in thrusting words having no connection with the subject into all parts of every sentence—Bootjack, for instance—wouldn't you think he was taking a liberty with you, and trifling with your time, and wasting his own?"

This student adds: "He then introduced the 'Bootjack' violently and frequently into a sentence, to illustrate the absurdity of street bad language in a striking way."

Despite the fact that "everyone in that school had their duties assigned, as on a Cunard steamer, and did their own part," with Henry the more rigid of the two schoolmasters, children caught him by the hand as he was going home from school, to walk with him and hear more. John had the younger students, Henry the older, whom he taught Latin and Greek and natural philosophy. Once a week both brothers took their pupils on a nature walk. To their great delight, Henry always led them, unerringly, to the places where Indian arrowheads lay under the soil.

In the summer of 1839, Henry and John went on an extended nature study trip of their own, with boat, guns and a tent. But before they left, a momentous event— momentous in both their lives—occurred: they fell in love with the same girl.

Chapter Four

The River Voyage

THERE were staying in the Thoreau house, as paying guests, a Mrs. Joseph Ward, widow of a Revolutionary War colonel, and her daughter Prudence, who painted flower pictures and was an amateur botanist. In July, 1839, when Henry was twenty-two, and his brother twenty-four, a niece of Mrs. Ward's came by coach from Scituate, Massachusetts, to visit her aunt. Her name was Ellen Devereux Sewall, and she was seventeen years old. She took her bonnet off; and the two brothers saw what a siren from the coast looked like.

Ellen Sewall had plentiful dark hair full of ringlets; a wide, calm brow; pensive eyes beautifully spaced, the lashes making soft shadows in the hollows above the high cheekbones; a classic nose almost a little too pointed at the tip; and a laughing mouth.

And John and Henry were lost—lost at once—at first sight—forever.

It was midsummer. School was closed. With spin-
sterish Prudence Ward acting as chaperone, but hardly
noticed, the two brothers squired Ellen Sewall everywhere—to the sights at a traveling circus, to the woods
surrounding Concord, to boat rides on the river. She
had arrived on July 20. On July 25 Henry was already
writing in his journal: "There is no remedy for love
but to love more." John neither said nor wrote anything. But he was just as much in love.

Ellen stayed three weeks. Then, as suddenly as she
had appeared, she was gone, leaving behind her poig-
nant memories and secret sighs. John and Henry said
nothing to each other about her. They resumed their
preparations for the river journey.

They had built their boat in the spring. Fifteen feet
long by three and a half in breadth at the widest
part, it was painted green, with a blue border. It had
two sets of oars, several slender poles for use in shal-
low places, and two masts, one of them made to serve
as a tent pole at night. Their tent was of heavy cotton
cloth, and they had buffalo skins to sleep on. To trun-
dle the boat around falls they had made a frame with
wheels. As Henry remarked: "If rightly made, a boat
would be a sort of amphibious animal, a creature of two
elements."

On the evening of August 30, 1839, which was a
Friday, Henry and John loaded their boat with utensils,
potatoes and melons grown by themselves, two guns, the

tent and the other equipment. The next day they launched the boat on the Concord River and set out, plying their oars. Some friends stood on a hill downstream to wave them good-by, but the two brothers glided past without looking up. They had already said good-by once; that sufficed. However, when they were out of sight, they let their oars drop, and taking up their guns, fired a salvo into the air as a parting salute.

Resting on their oars, they drifted past the first battleground of the Revolution, where Henry made out "the still visible abutments of that North Bridge over which in April, 1775, rolled the first faint tide of that war which ceased not, till, as we read on the stone on our right, it 'gave peace to these United States.' "

Concord was left behind. In the water, pickerel and bream flashed away from the fury of the oars; bitterns with booming voices rose ungainly from the shore and the long grass beyond; turtles slid into the water. Far off, in the meadows, the brothers saw farmers at their haying, "their heads waving like the grass which they cut."

After a voyage of about seven miles, Henry and John looked about for a place to pitch their tent and spend the night. They moored their boat to some high ground and there they made a meal off bread and sugar and cocoa. To make the cocoa, they boiled river water. Blackberries were ripe on the bushes, and made their dessert. The sun was going down as they put up their tent, and the landscape had taken on the mysterious aura of evening in the outdoors.

Through the triangular opening of the tent they could see a mast of their boat. They stayed awake a long time, hearing the strange sounds of the night—the scraping of leaves, the plashing of the water, an owl hooting far off. A fox prowled near the tent, stepping on dead leaves, and a muskrat nuzzled the potatoes and melons in the boat. When they left in the morning, they named their camping place "Fox Island."

A canal six miles long joined the Concord and Merrimack Rivers; one of the brothers ran along the towpath drawing the boat by a cord, while the other kept it from bumping the shore with a pole. Thus they reached Middlesex, and were let down into the Merrimack through the locks above Pawtucket Falls. Indians were much in Henry's mind as they resumed their rowing and steering:

"It was in fact an old battle and hunting ground through which we had been floating, the ancient dwelling place of a race of hunters and warriors. Their weirs of stone, their arrowheads and hatchets, their pestles, and the mortars in which they pounded Indian corn before the white man had tasted it, lay concealed in the mud of the river bottom."

It was Sunday; they heard the pleasant bells of
Chelmsford, where they had lived as children, ring-
ing out over the fields beyond the river. On their right,
between Chelmsford and Tyngsboro, Massachusetts,
lay Wicasuck Island, seventy acres or more, Henry
estimated. This island, he knew, had been a favorite
residence of the Indians. He had read that, "about
1663, the eldest son of Passaconaway (Chief of the
Penacooks), was thrown into jail for a debt of £45,
due to John Tinker, by one of his tribe, and which he
had promised verbally should be paid. To relieve him
from his imprisonment, his brother Wanalancet and
others, who owned Wicasuck Island, sold it and paid
the debt." The General Court afterwards restored it to
the Indians; but in 1683 they departed. The white man
was uncomfortably close.

Thus Sunday passed on the river, and at sundown the
brothers moored their boat on Tyngsboro shore. With
tent pitched, and the buffalo robes spread on the grass
for their bed—they had a blanket for cover—they hung
a lantern to the tent pole and built a fire near the en-
trance. After eating, they put out the blaze, closed the
tent flap, and disposed themselves to sleep, Henry first
making some notes for his journal. He could not fall
asleep for thinking of the mink, muskrats, field mice,
woodchucks, squirrels, skunks, rabbits, foxes, and
weasels, all of which were near, he knew. But it was

not an animal that disturbed them in the night. One of
the brothers had a nightmare; but Henry's account
of the trip does not make clear if it was himself or
John.

The next morning, in a rain of birdsong and the
cheerful sound of the river "rippling confidently seaward," one of the brothers—again, not clear which
—took the boat to the opposite shore. There, where the
ground was flat, he emptied it of water and washed out
the clay that had accumulated, while the other made a
fire and prepared breakfast. It was still dark when they
resumed their voyage.

They were in the territory of ancient Dunstable: "It
was from Dunstable, then a frontier town, that the famous Captain Lovewell, with his company, marched in
quest of the Indians on the 18th of April, 1725." Lovewell and his band met the Indians in the forest of
Pequawket. "A remnant returned home to enjoy the
fame of their victory." With a parting sigh, Henry
mourned the Indians, who had also suffered grievous
losses, and about whom the history he had read was
silent.

Chapter Five

The River Voyage (Concluded)

THEY were now in New Hampshire, their mother's state. As the long green boat with its blue border nosed farther and farther up the Merrimack, Henry made notes of the surrounding countryside.

"The river," he afterwards wrote, "was the only key which could unlock its maze, presenting its hills and valleys, its lakes and streams, in their natural order and position."

He told John what he knew about the Merrimack— that its other name was the Sturgeon River, and that it was formed by the confluence of Indian streams, the Pemigewasset, which rises in the White Mountains, and the Winnepesaukee which drains Lake Winnepesaukee, the name meaning "The Smile of the Great Spirit."

The brothers did not talk about Ellen Sewall, and Henry's account of the trip, though full of musings about love and friendship, does not mention her.

From time to time, as one of the brothers rowed, the other went ashore and across the fields to fetch water from a farmer's well. Children struggled for the best place at a window to see the stranger.

Returning from one of these side excursions, Henry discovered, by the riverside, the foundation of an Indian wigwam, "a perfect circle of burnt stones, four or five feet in diameter, mingled with fine charcoal, and the bones of small animals which had been preserved in the sand. The surrounding sand was sprinkled with other burnt stones on which their fires had been built, as well as flakes of arrowhead stone." He found "one perfect arrowhead." He thought of the vanished Redmen fishing there before the white man arrived.

Off the town of Hudson he and John stopped to bathe, and then reclined under some buttonwood trees. They saw muskrats and kingfishers.

The naturalist in Henry awoke at the sight of a new tree which overhung the water. It had a broad, rounded leaf interspersed with clusters of small, hard berries. It was *Tilia Americana*, the lime or linden tree, from whose inner bark, called the bast (or bass), baskets and matting are made. He soon learned more about it: "Its sap affords sugar, and the honey made from its flowers is said to be preferred to any other. Its leaves are in some countries given to cattle, a kind of chocolate has been made of its fruit, a medicine has been prepared from an infusion of its flowers, and finally, the

charcoal made of its wood is greatly valued for gun-
powder."

In truth, a mighty busy tree. It afforded Henry
numerous reflections: "Look up at the tree-tops, and
see how finely Nature finishes off her work there. . . .
Leaves are of more various forms than the alphabets
of all languages put together. . . ."

They had arrived at Salmon Brook, which joins the
Merrimack off Nashua, New Hampshire. "About one
mile up this stream stood the house of old John Lovewell, who was an ensign in the army of Oliver Crom-
well, and the father of 'famous Captain Lovewell,' "
he who had fought the Indians. Old John had lived to
be 120 years old!

After passing Nashua, they looked for a place to
moor their boat and pitch their tent. They made their
camp under the skirts of a pine wood, with pine needles
for carpet underfoot, and their buffalo robes for bed.
"Our cocoa was soon boiled, and supper set upon our
chest, and we lengthened out this meal like old voyageurs, with our talk." To the distant baying of a dog
and the nearer shrilling of crickets, they fell asleep.
"It was pleasant to lie with our heads so low in the
grass, and hear what a tinkling ever-busy laboratory
it was. A thousand little artisans beat on their anvils
all night long."

Hatchet in hand, long before daylight, the brothers

woke the woods with their chopping; a fire was built, and soon their kettle was singing merrily. Once more the boat was hauled up and turned upside down and washed out. They set off in the fog at three o'clock.

"The river became swifter, and the scenery more pleasing than before."

Villages were few and far between, and all they saw were alternate wood and pasture lands. No wonder the Indian crept into Henry's thoughts again, for now he could imagine the countryside in its primitive state. Overhead the fish hawk wheeled and screamed, and as he and John looked up to see the bird circling in the sky, closer at hand, on the branch of an overhanging tree, they saw a striped squirrel "twirling a green nut with one paw, as in a lathe, while the other held it fast against its incisors as chisels."

To Henry, this squirrel was "like an independent russet leaf, with a will of its own, rustling whither it could . . . now peeping at the voyageurs through a crack with only its tail visible, now at its lunch deep in the toothsome kernel, and now a rod off playing at hide-and-seek, with the nut stowed away in its chops, where were half a dozen more besides, extending its cheeks to a ludicrous breadth. . . . And now with a chuckling squeak it dives into the root of a hazel, and we see no more of it." Others, however, appeared, and the temptation of some fresh meat proved too great for John and Henry.

They stopped rowing and took up their guns. Both were good shots.

In the afternoon they stopped to rest on a large island with steep banks and groves of elm and oak. They built a fire, and began to skin the squirrels they had shot. Suddenly they looked at each other and threw them away. "Their small red bodies, little bundles of red tissue, mere gobbets of venison, would not have 'fattened fire.' " They washed their hands and boiled rice instead.

That afternoon, for the first time, they raised their sail, and for an hour or so let the southwest wind drive them along while the oars lay unused. And that night they slept on the mainland, in Bedford. In the morning, before it was light, they pushed off again. The smaller bittern, "the genius of the shore," watched the intruders with a sullen eye, or "ran along over the wet stones like a wrecker in his storm coat, looking out for wrecks of snails and cockles."

They saw the monument to General John Stark, who commanded a regiment of the New Hampshire militia at Bunker Hill and was the victor, in 1777, of the Battle of Bennington. The monument could be seen from afar—"it suggested," thought Henry, "how much more impressive in the landscape is the tomb of a hero than the dwellings of the inglorious living. Who is most dead?" he questioned, "a hero by whose monument you stand, or his descendants of whom you have never heard?" And again he regretted that the graves of two Indian chiefs who had been the white man's friends "are marked by no monument on the bank of their native river."

Above Amoskeag, the river broadened into a lake, where were many canal boats, such as those Henry had seen as a boy on the Concord River. They were bound for Hooksett, eight miles away; one of them offered to take the Thoreau boat in tow.

It turned out, however, that what the boatmen meant was, to take their boat on board. It was too heavy for that. So the Thoreaus crossed to the opposite shore, and after coming to anchor under some alders, took their lunch. One by one the canal boats went by with broad sails set. As the one that had offered a lift went by, the brothers were hailed—ironically; if they would come alongside now, it would take them in tow. The Thoreaus said nothing in reply. After lunch, they hoisted their own sail and shot rapidly up the stream, passing the canal boats one after the other. As they passed the one that had taunted them, "we returned their compliment by proposing, if they would throw us a rope, to 'take them in tow,' to which these Merrimack sailors had no suitable answer ready."

Five or six miles above Amoskeag, just before sunset, one of the brothers landed to look for a farmhouse

to replenish their stores, while the other cruised back and forth to find a suitable bivouac for the night. Together with a loaf of homemade bread, and musk and watermelon, the voyager who had gone inland brought back "a little flaxen-headed boy, with some tradition, or small edition, of Robinson Crusoe in his head, who had been charmed by the account of our adventures, and asked his father's leave to join us. He examined, at first from the top of the bank, our boat and furniture, with sparkling eyes, and wished himself already his own man. He was a lively and interesting boy, and we should have been glad to ship him; but Nathan was still his father's boy, and had not come to years of discretion." He took home, instead, his secret memories of the Thoreau boat and the river that now flowed in his thoughts to farther reaches than he had before imagined.

The brothers moored their boat at the mouth of a small brook on the opposite shore, setting one of the larger melons to cool in the water under the alder trees. The melon, or the water, had a will of its own; when their tent was pitched, they found the melon gone—it had floated out into the river, and out of sight. It was too valuable a property to be lost thus easily, and taking their boat, they went in pursuit. It was fast growing dark, but they soon discerned the melon gently floating seaward with a convoy of twigs and leaves. It tasted better for their exertions.

They awoke in the morning to the patter of rain on their tent. "We managed," says Henry, "to keep our thoughts dry, however." In the corn barn of the farmer from whom they had bought the melons, they hung their tent and buffalo robes to dry. Nathan watched with fascinated eyes. They had decided to go forward on foot. Henry said of this part of their excursion:

"We were hospitably entertained in Concord, New Hampshire, which we persisted in calling *New* Concord, as we had been wont, to distinguish it from our native town, from which we had been told that it was named and in part originally settled. This would have been the proper place to conclude our voyage, uniting Concord with Concord by these meandering rivers, but our boat was moored some miles below its port."

They returned to Hooksett and retrieved their equipment. The boat was safe in its harbor, where they had left it, and at noon, with a fair wind, and the current now in their favor, they began the return voyage.

One night marked the turning point of the season. "We had gone to bed in summer, and we awoke in autumn; for summer passes into autumn in some unimaginable point of time, like the turning of a leaf."

They passed the New Hampshire line and saw Tyngsboro once more, Wicasuck Island, and Chelmsford. "Thus thoughtfully we were rowing homeward to find some autumnal work to do, and help on the revolution of the seasons. Perhaps Nature would condescend to make use of us even without our knowledge, as when we help to scatter her seeds in our walks, and carry burrs and cockles on our clothes from field to field."

And thus they came back to Concord, each with his memories. Whatever Henry planned to do next, John's plans were already made. He rushed off to Scituate to visit Ellen Sewall. The significance of this could not have escaped Henry. But he said nothing. If that was the way things were, his beloved brother should have the first chance. Henry's ordeal must have been great. Ellen wrote Prudence Ward: "You don't know how much pleasure Mr. John's visit has afforded us." There was small comfort in a reference to Henry. Emerson had edited the American edition of Carlyle's *Sartor Resartus*. Henry had sent it, or recommended it, to Ellen. Her comment was: "What a queer book!"

It was fortunate for Henry that he had the Parkman House school to occupy his thoughts that fall; but after school, on his solitary walks in the woods, a spirit walked by his side, the spirit of Ellen Sewall with her bonnet and ringlets. He never discussed her with John; and John was equally silent about the image and the dream that brightened both their minds.

Both brothers accompanied Prudence Ward to Scitu-

ate in December. Ellen's father looked them over with
a stern, nineteenth-century eye. The following June,
Ellen came again to Concord, and Henry took her boat-
ing on the river. John gave her stones for her mineral
collection. In July, John went once more to Scituate.
There, walking on the beach with Ellen, he proposed and
was accepted. But her mother and father were both
against the match, and she broke off the engagement.
This, Henry felt, released him from his silence. He
wrote to Ellen. And he wrote in his journal: "August
7. A wave of happiness flows over me."

The wave broke shortly against the hard rock of
Papa Sewall's wrath. Henry had proposed in his turn,
and a letter from Ellen to her aunt tells the result:

"Father. . . . wished me to write immediately in a
short, explicit and cold manner to Mr. T. . . . I wrote
to H. T. that evening. I never felt so badly at sending
a letter in my life."

It does not appear that she was in love with Henry,
for she adds: "I do feel so sorry H. wrote to me. It was
such a pity. Though I would rather have it so than to
have him say the same things on the *beach* or anywhere
else."

She married elsewhere; a daguerreotype of her with
three of her children shows her beautiful and pensive
in maturity. She forgot about the Thoreaus. But Henry

never forgot her. He confessed before he died that she was never out of his thoughts. His shattering experience at twenty-three gave direction to his life, for it confirmed him in his bachelorhood, to which his oddities inclined him, and turned his ardent spirit to worship at the shrine of Nature. He wrote in his journal: "To sigh under the cold, cold moon for a love unrequited is but a slight on nature; the natural remedy would be to fall in love with the moon and the night and find our love requited."

As for John, in the fall of 1841 he began to show alarming symptoms of tuberculosis, a disease which ran in the Thoreau family. Perhaps the emotional experience he had undergone over Ellen had weakened his powers of resistance. Early in 1842 he cut himself accidentally; tetanus (lockjaw) set in, and he died in agony.

Thus ended a momentous period in the life of Henry Thoreau.

"I feel as if years had been crowded into the last month," he wrote in his journal.

Chapter Six

In Emerson's House

HENRY THOREAU'S ordeal had not escaped the observation of his friend Emerson. The death of John Thoreau had put an end to the school run by the two brothers; Henry could not or would not run it by himself. He was at loose ends. And he was plainly unhappy.

Ralph Waldo Emerson, who was to become world-renowned as the sage of Concord, had been watching Henry's growth as an original thinker and writer—he had read Henry's journal, as well as the poems he was writing, and had been much impressed by the young man's pine-fresh thoughts and style. His own journal is full of their meetings, and of the tonic effect on himself of their walks and talks: "I delight much in my young friend, who seems to have as free and erect a mind as any I have ever met." Fourteen years older than Thoreau, Emerson was the descendant of eight generations of ministers, one of them a founder of Concord. He had himself been ordained, but withdrew from the ministry to pursue a life of authorship.

In appearance, he was much like Thoreau, though thinner, frailer. His head, for all that it was full of great thoughts that were to stir his countrymen, was small; under its mass of hair, swept neatly to one side, flanked by long sideburns, piercing eyes looked out at the world over a generous Yankee nose. His mouth, which appeared prim at first glance was, on a second one, seen to be humorous, too humorous, some thought. When he smiled, he closed his eyes.

Had Henry been any older, Emerson might have seen in him only a rival, for their thinking and attitude towards life were similar. To some extent, even Henry's style and direction stemmed from the older man's philosophy, especially from the little book—it was less than a hundred pages—entitled *Nature,* which Emerson had published in 1836. In 1837 he had given the famous lecture, "The American Scholar," before the Phi Beta Kappa society at Harvard. After more than a hundred years it remains the most memorable talk ever given before that august body. The goal of truth, he had declared, is character—"a great soul will be strong to live as well as strong to think."

Such was the man who, perceiving that a crisis had appeared in Thoreau's life, generously went to his res-

cue. He knew, of course, that he could not approach
this proud, hurt, diffident and difficult young man with
an offer of help. It would have been spurned. He asked
Henry to help *him*! Occupied with his books, his lectures, his garden, his family, and in poor health, Emerson needed assistance, he said, and offered Henry his
board for whatever work he chose to do. It was a forth-
right proposal, and Henry accepted it. He was glad to
get away from the Thoreau house with its memories. He
moved in.

Emerson wrote to his friend Thomas Carlyle in
England:

"One reader and friend of yours dwells now in my
house, and, as I hope, for twelve months to come—
Henry Thoreau—a poet whom you may one day be
proud of—a noble, manly youth, full of melodies and
inventions. We work together day by day in my garden,
and I grow well and strong."

Shortly, Henry was looking after the garden by
himself. He was also handy with carpenter's tools, and
found chores around the Emerson house. He got Mrs.
Emerson to make "shoes" of thin morocco for the hens
to keep them from scratching up the garden. He became the companion of the Emerson children, playing
with them outdoors, making toys for them, reading to
them and telling stories. (We will come later to Ed-

ward Waldo Emerson's reminiscences of his father's friend.) But still, whenever he could, he slipped away from family and house to walk in the fields and woods. In a notebook which had belonged to his brother John, Henry wrote of himself about this time:

"I am about five feet 7 inches in height—of a light complexion, rather slimly built, and just approaching the Roman age of manhood [twenty-five]. One who faces West oftener than East—walks out of the house with a better grace than he goes in—who loves winter as well as summer—forest as well as field—darkness as well as light. Rather solitary than gregarious—not migratory, nor dormant—but to be raised at any season, by day or night, not by the pulling of any bell wire, but by a smart stroke upon any pine tree in the woods of Concord."

The Emersons, he was saying in effect, if only to himself at this time, were not going to domesticate *him*. Thus he appeared to himself; and about the time that he was writing his own description, another was writing how he looked to an outsider.

Nathaniel Hawthorne, who came to Concord in July, 1842, had observed Thoreau as he was putting the garden of the "Old Manse" in order—it was done at Emerson's suggestion. Hawthorne wrote in *his* notebook:

"Mr. Thoreau is a singular character; a young man with much of wild, original Nature still remaining in him; and so far as he is sophisticated, it is in a way and method of his own. He is ugly as sin; long-nosed, queer-mouthed, and with uncouth and somewhat rustic, although courteous manners, corresponding very well with such an exterior. But his ugliness is of an honest and agreeable fashion, and becomes him much better than beauty."

Although the Puritan in Hawthorne made him add, "For two or three years back, he has repudiated all regular modes of getting a living, and seems inclined to lead a sort of Indian life," he gave credit where credit was due. He had seen almost at once that Thoreau was "a keen and delicate observer of Nature." He rounded off his portrait thus:

"Nature, in return for his love, seems to adopt him as her especial child; and shows him secrets which few others are allowed to witness. He is familiar with beast, fish, fowl and reptile, and has strange stories to tell of adventures and friendly passages with these lower brethren of mortality. Herb and flower, likewise, wherever they grow, whether in garden or wildwood, are his familiar friends. He is on intimate terms with the clouds also, and can tell the portents of storms. He has a great regard for the memory of the Indian tribes, whose wild life would have suited him so well; and, strange to say, he seldom walks over a plowed field without picking up an arrow-point, spearhead, or other relic of the red man."

They had gone on walks together, and later, in the winter, they skated together on the river. Emerson made a third. Henry, who was an expert on skates, danced and leaped over the ice; Hawthorne, in a long cloak, moved more slowly, "stately and grave"; while Emerson slid about head foremost, "half lying on the air." Henry, it would appear, was the only one who was really at home outdoors.

To Hawthorne he was now one of the few persons "with whom to hold intercourse is like hearing the wind among the boughs of a forest-tree; and with all this wild freedom, there is high and classic cultivation in him, too."

There were literary gatherings in the Emerson house at night, and Henry made a shy member of the group, self-conscious perhaps in his homespun clothes, which made him look like a farmer among the genteel-spoken, well-dressed, and famous authors. But he occasionally startled them with his direct observations and speech:

"Poetry cannot breathe in the scholar's atmosphere."

"I find incessant labor with the hands, which en-

grosses the attention also, the best method to remove palaver out of one's style."

He had been assisting his father in the pencil factory as well as doing chores for the Emersons. But little by little the resolution to strike out for himself, in his own particular way, grew in him. Soon he was writing in his journal: "There is in my nature, methinks, a singular yearning towards all wildness."

It was at this juncture that destiny took a hand.

In October, 1844, Emerson had been offered the opportunity to buy a field comprising some eleven acres for $8.10 per acre. The field was in a pine wood above Walden Pond. After he had bought it, Thoreau told him that if the owner of the adjacent pine grove cut it down, the eleven acres would have less value—as woodland, of course, not mere real estate. So Emerson bought the pine grove of three or four acres for $125 more. He wrote to his brother on Staten Island: "I am landlord and water-lord of 14 acres, more or less, on the shore of Walden, and can raise my own blackberries."

The harvest was to be greater than that—an American experience which has stirred the imaginations of men in many lands, and an American book which ranks high in the select library of world literature. It was Emerson's encouragement, as well as the bent of his own genius, that turned Thoreau's thoughts towards

Walden Pond. The town had long referred to the two men scoffingly as "the walkers." Famous and respected, Emerson escaped severer censure; Thoreau, however, had as yet achieved practically nothing—according to Concord. But he himself had an entirely different opinion:

"How many mornings, summer and winter, before yet any neighbor was stirring about his business, have I been about mine! No doubt, many of my townsmen have met me returning from this enterprise, farmers starting for Boston in the twilight, or woodchoppers going to their work. It is true, I never assisted the sun materially in his rising, but, doubt not, it was of the last importance only to be present at it.

"So many autumn, ay, and winter days, spent outside the town, trying to hear what was in the wind, to hear and carry it express! I well-nigh sunk all my capital in it, and lost my own breath into the bargain, running in the face of it. If it had concerned either of the political parties, depend upon it, it would have appeared in the *Gazette* with the earliest intelligence."

Chapter Seven

Walden

IN 1845, Polk was President. The United States had pushed its borders west to the Pacific and south to the Rio Grande. Oregon and Texas entered the Union. War almost came with England over Oregon; it came with Mexico over Texas. Wagon trails began to be visible in the tall grass where the bearded buffalo roamed in vast herds. Would the new states be slave or free? The issue, which was to lead to civil war, was already in the open, dividing communities and families.

For all this—except that he was against slavery, as he was against meanness of any kind—Thoreau cared nothing. What he cared about he has told with passionate intensity. He lived by the shore of Walden Pond for two years and two months, from July 4, 1845, to September 6, 1847. Out of his work and walks, out of his solitude and thoughts, came *Walden*, a book as original as the man himself.

"I went to the woods," he wrote in it, "because I wished to live deliberately, to front only the essential facts of life, and see if I could not learn what it had to teach, and not, when I came to die, discover that I had not lived. I did not wish to live what was not life, living is so dear; nor did I wish to practice resignation, unless it was quite necessary. I wanted to live deep and suck out all the marrow of life, to live so sturdily and Spartan-like as to put to rout all that was not life, to cut a broad swath and shave close, to drive life into a corner, and reduce it to its lowest terms, and, if it proved to be mean, why then to get the whole and genuine meanness of it, and publish its meanness to the world; or if it were sublime, to know it by experience, and be able to give a true account of it in my next excursion."

He had found a way of life—a way to live that suited him—and the means by which to live it. He had had the satisfaction of building his own house. True, it was not very large; but had he wished for more accommodation, he would have added to it. The land was not his; but he had improved it for Emerson by clearing out briars and planting crops. His wants were few and simple ones; he lived, mainly, on rice, rye and Indian meal (without yeast), potatoes, a little salt pork, and molasses.

"It was fit," he declared, "that I should live on rice, mainly, who loved so well the philosophy of India."

When blueberries or huckleberries were ripe he made a meal off them and brought back a store for other days: "The fruits do not yield their true flavor to the purchaser of them."

He sometimes supplemented his basic diet with fish that he caught in Walden Pond, and he has confessed that once he went so far as to slaughter a woodchuck which ravaged his bean field. "It afforded me a momentary enjoyment, notwithstanding a musky flavor." He saw, however, "that the longest use would not make that a good practice, however it might seem to have your woodchucks ready dressed by the village butcher." To protect his bean field from the ravages of woodchucks, he set up a trap; but when he found one in it, he carried it two miles away and set it free. He had long before developed scruples against killing wild things; he no longer had a gun, and except on a few occasions, refrained even from fishing. He drank only water—no coffee, no tea; and, of course, no spirituous liquors.

At first he made bread out of Indian meal and salt —"genuine hoe-cakes," he called them, baked in an outdoor fire at the end of a piece of wood; but the pitch-pine that he burned not only smoked them up but gave them a piney flavor. He finally found a mixture of rye and Indian meal best for his purposes, baking several small loaves in succession in a pan, and wrapping them in cloth the better to keep. But sometimes he went without bread. "At one time," he has recorded, "owing to the emptiness of my purse, I saw none of it for more than a month."

He found afterwards that his food came to $8.74 for the first eight months. During the same period he earned, by day labor, such as surveying and carpentry, $13.34; and from time to time, after a visit to his mother, he returned to Walden Pond with, it may be, a loaf of bread or a pie. He also dined occasionally with Emerson. The best part, for him, of these excursions into town came when he wended his way back to his hut, feeling the familiar trail with his feet and looking at the stars through latticed branches overhead. He had no envy of those who had more than he:

"One evening I overtook one of my townsmen, who has accumulated what is called a handsome property —though I never got a *fair* view of it—on the Walden road, driving a pair of cattle to market, who inquired of me how I could bring my mind to give up so many of the comforts of life. I answered that I was very sure that I liked it passably well; I was not joking. And so I went home to my bed and left him to pick his way through the darkness and the mud to Brighton

—or Bright-town—which place he would reach some time in the morning."

He awoke each day to the myriad songs of birds, the lapping of lake water, the wind in the pines. He started the day with a dip in the pond. He hoed, he read, and he wrote, sitting at his three-legged table, in his journal. "Nay, I often did better than this," he tells. "There were times when I could not afford to sacrifice the bloom of the present moment to any work, whether of the head or hands. I love a broad margin to my life. Sometimes, in a summer morning, having taken my accustomed bath, I sat in my sunny doorway from sunrise till noon, rapt in a revery amidst the pines and hickories and sumachs, in undisturbed solitude and stillness, while the birds sang around or flitted noiseless through the house, until by the sun falling in at my west window, or the noise of some traveller's wagon on the distant highway, I was reminded of the lapse of time. I grew in those seasons like corn in the night, and they were far better than any work of the hands would have been. They were not time subtracted from my life, but so much over and above my usual allowance."

One day he was witness of a Homeric battle:

"When I went out to my wood-pile, or rather my pile of stumps, I observed two large ants, the one red, the other much larger, nearly half an inch long, and black, fiercely contending with one another. Having once got hold they never let go, but struggled and wrestled and rolled on the chips incessantly. Looking farther, I was surprised to find that the chips were covered with such combatants, that it was not a duellum [duel], but a bellum [war], a war between two races of ants, the red always pitted against the black, and frequently two red ones to one black. The legions of these Myrmidons covered all the hills and vales in my wood-yard, and the ground was already strewn with the dead and dying, both red and black . . . .

"On every side they were engaged in deadly combat, yet without any noise that I could hear, and human soldiers never fought so resolutely. I watched a couple that were fast locked in each other's embraces, in a little sunny valley amid the chips, now at noonday prepared to fight till the sun went down, or life went out. The smaller red champion had fastened himself like a vice to his adversary's front, and through all the tumblings on that field never for an instant ceased to gnaw at one of his feelers near the root, having already caused the other to go by the board; while the stronger black one dashed him from side to side, and, as I saw on looking nearer, had already divested him of several of his members. They fought with more pertinacity than bulldogs. Neither manifested the least disposition to retreat. It was evident that their battle-cry was 'Conquer or die.'

"In the meanwhile there came along a single red ant on the hillside of this valley, evidently full of excitement, who either had despatched his foe, or had not yet taken part in the battle; probably the latter, for he had lost none of his limbs; whose mother had charged him to return with his shield or upon it. Or perchance he was some Achilles, who had nourished his wrath apart, and had now come to avenge or rescue his Patroclus. He saw this unequal combat from afar —for the blacks were nearly twice the size of the red—he drew near with rapid pace till he stood on his guard within half an inch of the combatants; then, watching his opportunity, he sprang upon the black warrior, and commenced his operations near the root of his right foreleg, leaving the foe to select among his own members; and so there were three united for life, as if a new kind of attraction had been invented which put all other locks and cements to shame. I should not have wondered by this time to find that they had their respective musical bands stationed on some eminent chip, and playing their national airs the while, to excite the slow and cheer the dying combatants.

"I was myself excited somewhat even as if they had been men. The more you think of it, the less the difference. And certainly there is not the fight recorded in

Concord history, at least, if in the history of America,
that will bear a moment's comparison with this, whether
for the numbers engaged in it, or for the patriotism
and heroism displayed. For numbers and for carnage
it was an Austerlitz or Dresden. Concord Fight! Two
killed on the patriots' side, and Luther Blanchard
wounded! Why here every ant was a Buttrick—'Fire!
for God's sake fire!'—and thousands shared the fate
of Davis and Hosmer. There was not one hireling
there. I have no doubt that it was a principle they
fought for, as much as our ancestors, and not to avoid
a three-penny tax on their tea; and the results of this
battle will be as important and memorable to those
whom it concerns as those of the battle of Bunker Hill,
at least."

He sunned himself within and without; and he also
sunned his house: "Housework was a pleasant pastime.
When my floor was dirty, I rose early, and setting all
my furniture out of doors on the grass, bed and bed-
stead making but one budget, dashed water on the floor,
and sprinkled white sand from the pond on it, and
then with a broom scrubbed it clean and white; and
by the time the villagers had broken their fast the
morning sun had dried my house sufficiently to allow
me to move in again, and my meditations were almost
uninterrupted. It was pleasant to see my whole household effects out on the grass, making a little pile like

a gypsy's pack, and my three-legged table, from which I did not remove the books and pen and ink, standing amid the pines and hickories. They seemed glad to get out themselves, and as if unwilling to be brought in."

He was tempted to leave them out and spread an awning over them and sit at his desk under the trees.

But even inside he was not far removed from the life of the open. From his window he could see hawks circling above the clearing he had made; a tantivy, or rush, of wild pigeons; a fish hawk dimpling the glassy surface of the pond and then bringing up a fish; or a mink stealing out of the marsh and seizing a frog. A blue jay screamed, the sedge bent under the weight of reedbirds flitting to and fro, the branches dipped and swayed to alighting songbirds. A loon laughed from the pond, a fox barked; and regularly, within five minutes of sunset, the whippoorwill—sometimes four or five—muttered strenuous notes for half an hour. After them came the screech owls and the hooting owls, making the night mournful with their wails.

On Sundays, he heard the church bells of Lincoln, Acton, Bedford, and Concord, faint and far, "and, as it were, natural melody, worth importing to the wilderness."

He set up his own sounds, his own music, in reply:

"When, as was commonly the case, I had none to commune with, I used to raise the echoes by striking with a paddle on the side of my boat, filling the surrounding woods with circling and dilating sound, stirring them up as a keeper of a menagerie his wild beasts, until I elicited a growl from every wooded vale and hillside.

"In warm evenings I frequently sat in the boat playing the flute, and saw the perch, which I seem to have charmed, hovering around me, and the moon travelling over the ribbed bottom, which was strewed with the wrecks of the forest."

He could not get enough of the pond:

"Sometimes, after staying in a village parlor till the family had all retired, I have returned to the woods, and partly with a view to the next day's dinner, spent the hours of midnight fishing from a boat by moonlight, serenaded by owls and foxes, and hearing, from time to time, the creaking note of some unknown bird close at hand. These experiences were very memorable and valuable to me—anchored in forty feet of water, and twenty or thirty rods [a rod is 16½ feet] from the shore, surrounded sometimes by thousands of small perch and shiners, dimpling the surface with their tails in the moonlight, and communicating by a long flaxen line with mysterious nocturnal fishes which had their dwelling forty feet below, or sometimes dragging sixty feet of line about the pond as I drifted in the gentle night breeze, now and then feeling a slight vibration along it, indicative of some life prowling about its extremity, of dull uncertain blundering purpose there, and slow to make up its mind. . . ."

Thus the pond by night. By day it mirrored not only the surrounding landscape but his own thoughts. "A lake," he wrote, "is the landscape's most beautiful and expressive feature. It is earth's eye; looking into which the beholder measures the depth of his own nature."

A field mouse had built its nest under his house. Regularly, at lunch time, it came out to nibble the crumbs at his feet. Thoreau thought it had never seen a man before. "It soon became quite familiar, and would run over my shoes and up my clothes." One day it tried a more perilous perch, on his sleeve, and then "round and round the paper which held my dinner, while I kept the latter close, and dodged and played at bopeep with it; and when at last I held still a piece of cheese between my thumb and finger, it came and nibbled it, sitting in my hand, and afterward cleaned its face and paws, like a fly, and walked away."

A phoebe built a nest in his woodshed. A robin nested in a pine close to the house. A partridge led her brood past his window, a stately procession from the woods in the rear of the house to the front, "clucking and calling to them like a hen, and in all her behavior proving herself the hen of the woods." He observed how the young suddenly dispersed at a signal from the mother, "as if a whirlwind had swept them away," lying still and squat, heads under leaves, and not moving except at the mother's signal given from a distance. "These were my hens and chickens."

He had human visitors. His reception of them varied: "Many a traveller came out of his way to see me and the inside of my house, and, as an excuse for calling, asked for a glass of water. I told them that I drank at the pond, and pointed thither, offering to lend them a dipper."

He noticed differences: "Girls and boys and young women generally seemed glad to be in the woods. They looked in the pond and at the flowers, and improved their time. Men of business, even farmers, thought only of solitude and employment, and of the great distance at which I dwelt from something or other; and though they said that they loved a ramble in the woods occasionally, it was obvious that they did not."

He was aware that when he was absent from his hut, there were prying eyes and hands: "How came Mrs. —— to know that my sheets were not as clean as hers?"

For the real bores he had a jingle. They "thought that I was forever singing—

'This is the house that I built;
This is the man that lives in the house that I built;'

but they did not know that the third line was—

'These are the folks that worry the man
That lives in the house that I built.' "

Children he put at the head of his list of "cheering
visitors"—"children come a-berrying, railroad men
taking a Sunday morning walk in clean shirts, fisher-
men and hunters, poets and philosophers; in short, all
honest pilgrims, who came out to the woods for freedom's sake, and really left the village behind."

Thus the days passed. The year turned. Across the
pond three maples turned scarlet, whispering of winter.
After building his chimney, Thoreau plastered the
walls. His house was now snug, and a fire glowed
cheerfully on the hearth. Outside, "the wind began to
howl around the house as if it had not had permission
to do so till then." Gaggles of geese passed over, bound
for Mexico. Snow covered the ground, and then the
pond froze.

He collected dead wood in the forest, bringing it to
the hut in his arms and on his shoulders, sometimes
trailing a dead tree under each arm over the snow.
"An old forest fence which had seen its best days was
a great haul for me," he recalled. On the other side of
the pond there was a raft of pitch pine logs; he slid
this, piecemeal, across the half mile of ice, skating
behind, sometimes with the end of a fifteen-foot log on
one shoulder, the other on the ice. He now had "an old

axe which nobody claimed." He was twice warmed
by his logs—"once while I was splitting them, and
again when they were on the fire."

Despite the cold, he went on his daily walks. But now
he seldom met anyone, except those who came to cut
wood and sled it to the village: "The elements, however,
abetted me in making a path through the deepest snow
in the woods, for when I had once gone through the
wind blew the oak leaves into my tracks, where they
lodged, and by absorbing the rays of the sun melted
the snow, and so not only made a dry bed for my feet,
but in the night their dark line was my guide."

For while he had no visitors for a week or a fort-
night at a time, he still continued to venture outdoors:
"I frequently tramped eight or ten miles through the
deepest snow to keep an appointment with a beech tree,
or a yellow birch, or an old acquaintance among the
pines." He also slid or skated on the pond, which was
his "yard." Sometimes, to get water, he took his axe
and cut through a foot of snow and then a foot of ice,
to "open a window under my feet, where, kneeling to
drink, I look down into the quiet parlor of the fishes,
pervaded by a softened light as through a window of
ground glass, with its bright sanded floor the same as
in summer."

He found that the ice was a noisy but sensitive in-
strument foretelling a change of temperature: "The

pond began to boom about an hour after sunrise, when it felt the influence of the sun's rays slanted upon it from over the hills; it stretched itself and yawned like a waking man with a gradually increasing tumult, which was kept up three or four hours. It took a short siesta at noon, and boomed once more toward night, as the sun was withdrawing its influence. In the right stage of the weather a pond fires its evening gun with great regularity . . . though I may perceive no difference in the weather, it does. Who would have suspected so large and cold and thick-skinned a thing to be so sensitive?"

The days grew longer; he saw that he would get through the winter without having to add to his wood-pile. He was now "on the alert for the first signs of spring, to hear the chance note of some arriving bird, or the striped squirrel's chirp, for his stores must be now exhausted, or see the woodchuck venture out of his winter quarters."

"One attraction," he wrote, "in coming to the woods to live was that I should have leisure and opportunity to see the Spring come in." By March 13 he had already heard the bluebird, song sparrow and redwing. After a few warm days, although there was still snow on the ground, he saw with pleasure "the first tender signs of the infant year"—life-everlasting, goldenrod, pinweed, wool-grass, cotton-grass, cat-tails, mulleins, johnswort, hardhack, meadowsweet—"bring back the summer to our winter memories." He watched the unfolding ferns. "Nature made ferns for pure leaves, to show what she could do in that line."

But it was the birds that lifted his heart. "The bluebird," he wrote, "carries the sky on its back." He was grateful for the commoner varieties:

"The first sparrow of spring! The year beginning with younger hope than ever! The faint silvery warblings heard over the partially bare and moist fields from the bluebird, the song sparrow, and the redwing, as if the last flakes of winter tinkled as they fell! What at such a time are histories, chronologies, traditions, and all written revelations? The brooks sing carols and glees to the spring. The marsh hawk, sailing low over the meadow, is already seeking the first slimy life that awakes. The sinking sound of melting snow is heard in all dells, and the ice dissolves apace in the ponds. The grass flames up on the hill sides like a spring fire."

He turned to watch the pond. There was now a canal more than thirty feet wide in the ice, and it was "glorious to behold this ribbon of water sparkling in the sun." Even when he was indoors he was aware of the pond and its steady transformation: "Suddenly an influx of light filled my house, though the evening was at hand, and the clouds of winter still overhung it, and the eaves were dripping with sleety rain. I looked out the window, and lo! where yesterday was cold gray ice there lay the transparent pond already calm and full of hope as in a summer evening, reflecting a summer evening sky in its bosom, though none was visible overhead, as if it had intelligence with some remote horizon.

"I heard a robin in the distance."

Chapter Eight

Thoreau and the Fugitive Slave

ON A summer afternoon, Thoreau set out for Concord. Blueberries were ripe, and he would have preferred to stay in the woods and pick them; but he had left a shoe at the cobbler's, and this was the errand that took him to town.

It was a momentous appearance. A few townsmen glanced at his familiar figure, some perhaps with an inward shrug of their thoughts, disapprovingly; but one approached him. He was Sam Staples, a bearded, shrewd, genial elder of the village who happened to be constable, jailor and tax collector.

"I'll pay your tax, Henry, if you're hard up," he said.

Thoreau had not paid his poll tax. He had not paid it because he disapproved of Massachusetts' stand on slavery and its adherence to the Fugitive Slave Act. Thoreau was not alone in this sentiment. By the 1840's many Northerners had become outraged by the pitiless tracking down of runaway slaves, and had begun to assist them, by means of the "Underground Railroad," to reach Canada and freedom. Several years before, Bronson Alcott had likewise refused to pay his poll tax, and had been arrested.

Thoreau, confronted with the alternative of paying up, or being arrested, chose the latter. There was nothing Staples could do, under existing law, but lead Thoreau to the village jail.

" 'Twas nothin' but principle," Staples afterwards said, after his offer to pay the tax himself had been turned down. He added: "I wouldn't have done it for old man Alcott."

When Staples and Thoreau arrived at the jail, the other prisoners were chatting and enjoying the evening air in the doorway.

"Come, boys," said Staples; "it is time to lock up."

In they went, to their respective cells.

Thoreau found that he had a cellmate.

"A first-rate fellow and a clever man," said Staples to Thoreau about his fellow prisoner, who had been accused of burning a barn.

"But I never did it," he told Thoreau when they were alone.

After the door was locked, he showed Henry where

to hang his hat. The door was of wood and iron, about a foot thick.

The room was simply furnished; the walls of solid stone, two or three feet thick, were whitewashed on the inside, giving the room a neat appearance. There was iron grating on the windows.

"I could not help being struck with the foolishness of that institution [the State] which treated me as if I were mere flesh and blood and bones, to be locked up," Thoreau afterwards recorded. "I wondered that it should have concluded at length that this was the best use it could put me to, and had never thought to avail itself of my services in some way. I saw that, if there was a wall of stone between me and my townsmen, there was a still more difficult one to climb or break through before they could get to be as free as I was. I did not for a moment feel confined, and the walls seemed a great waste of stone and mortar. I felt as if I alone of all my townsmen had paid my tax."

After listening to all the jail gossip that his cellmate could supply, Thoreau blew out the lamp, stretched himself on his bed, and fell asleep. In the morning, breakfast was handed in through a hole in the door on oblong tin pans. It consisted of a pint of chocolate and brown bread.

He was now free to go; for the night before, a woman with a shawl over her head—possibly Mrs. Emerson, possibly Thoreau's mother or his Aunt Maria—had appeared at the jail door and paid Henry's poll tax and fees to little Ellen Staples, the jailor's daughter. Old Sam was out, and returned too late to be told that someone had come "and paid Mr. Thoreau's tax." Ellen did not recognize the woman in the dark.

It was a custom in Concord to greet someone who had just come out of jail with crossed fingers, to represent the grating of a jail window; but no one saluted him thus; the passersby only looked at him and then at one another, "as if," as he said, "I had returned from a long journey." He was criticized by some for letting his tax be paid; but how could he help that? He was also criticized for leaving the jail; but of course Staples could not and would not keep him there, once the tax was paid. There is no satisfying everyone.

It will be recalled that Thoreau had gone into town to pick up his mended shoe. As though nothing had intervened, he went directly from the jail to the cobbler's, got his shoe, and returned to the woods to pick blueberries! "And then," he wrote, "the State was nowhere to be seen."

He had not, to be sure, settled the question of slavery; and now it came to his own doorstep. A fugitive Negro came cowering to the hut by Walden Pond. Thoreau fed him, helped him bathe his swollen feet, and told him he must think of nothing but rest.

"Have no fear," he told his visitor, "that any power should again wrong you."

Instead of going into the woods that day, he remained at home guarding his guest, until the fugitive could go forward, "toward the north star."

Chapter Nine

With Emerson's Children

THOREAU left Walden on September 6, 1847. In the bean field he had hoed so hard he planted pines. Nature returned like a green tide to drown the clearing he had made. He afterwards wrote:

"I left the woods for as good a reason as I went there. Perhaps it seemed to me that I had several more lives to live, and could not spare any more time for that one. . . .

"I learned this, at least, by my experiment: that if one advances confidently in the direction of his dreams, and endeavors to live the life which he has imagined, he will meet with a success unexpected in common hours."

He was too honest to pretend that his "experiment" had been nothing but undiluted joy, for he also noted in his journal: "There was a little stagnation, it may be. About 2 o'clock in the afternoon the world's axle creaked as if it needed greasing."

He sold the hut he had built to Emerson. The philosopher of Concord now asked him to live in his house again. Emerson was going to England to lecture, and he wished to have someone he could trust to look after his affairs. This time, Thoreau was to come, not merely as handyman, but as head of the household. In late September or early October, he took up his residence there in a room at the head of the stairs. Emerson sailed in October.

Emerson's son Edward afterwards recalled: "I can remember Mr. Thoreau as early as I can remember anybody, excepting my parents, my sisters, and my nurse. He had the run of our house, and on two occasions was man of the house during my father's long absences. He was to us children the best kind of an older brother. He soon became the guide and companion of our early expeditions afield, and, later, the advisor of our first camping trips."

He enlarged the portrait: "In childhood I had a friend—not a house friend, domestic, stuffy in association; nor yet herdsman, or horseman, or farmer, or slave of bench, or shop, or office; nor of letters, nor art, nor society; but a free, friendly, youthful-seeming man, who wandered in from unknown woods or fields without knocking—

'Between the night and day
When the fairy king has power'—

as the ballad says, passed by the elders' doors, but
straightway sought out the children, brightened up
the wood-fire forthwith; and it seemed as if it were the
effect of a wholesome brave north-wind, more than of
the armful of 'cat-sticks' which he would bring in from
the yard . . . when he, like the 'Pied Piper of Hamelin,'
sounded his note in the hall, the children must needs
come and hug his knees, and he struggled with them,
nothing loath, to the fireplace, sat down and told stories,
sometimes of the strange adventures of his childhood,
or more often of squirrels, muskrats, hawks, he had
seen that day, the Monitor-and-Merrimac duel of mud-
turtles in the river, or the great Homeric battle of the
red and black ants. Then he would make our pencils
and knives disappear, and redeem them presently from
our ears and noses; and last, would bring down the
heavy copper warming-pan from the oblivion of the
garret and unweariedly shake it over the blaze till
reverberations arose within, and then opening it, let a
white-blossoming explosion of popcorn fall over the
little people on the rug."

Thoreau also took the "little people" into the woods,
and on boat rides on the river. Edward Emerson recalled: "As the children grew older, he led them to
choice huckleberry hills, swamps where the great high-

bush blueberries grew, guided to the land of the chest-
nut and barberry, and more than all, opened that land
of enchantment into which, among dark hemlocks,
blood-red maples, and yellowing birches, we floated in
his boat, and freighted it with leaves and blue gentians
and fragrant grapes from the festooning vines."

They had also built a house of boughs on one of the
nearer hills, and lived on berries and beans, "happy as
the gods on Olympus."

Thoreau himself has left a glimpse of his stay in the
famous house behind the white picket fence. When
Ellen Emerson, the oldest child, was ten she went to
visit her relatives on Staten Island. He wrote to her as
follows:

"Dear Ellen—
"I think that we are pretty well acquainted, though
we never had any very long talks. We have had a good
many short talks, at any rate. Don't you remember
how we used to despatch our breakfasts two winters
ago, as soon as Eddy could get on his feeding-tire,
which was not always remembered before the rest of
the household had come down? Don't you remember
our wise criticisms on the pictures in the portfolio
and the Turkish book, with Eddy and Edith looking
on—how almost any pictures answered our purpose
and we went through the *Penny Magazine,* first from
beginning to end, and then from end to beginning, and

Eddy stared just as much the second time as the first, and Edith thought that we turned over too soon, and that there were some things which she had not seen? . . .

"Eddy has got him a fish-pole and line with a pin-hook at the end, which he flourishes over the dry ground and the carpet at the risk of tearing out our eyes; but when I told him that he must have a cork and a sinker, his mother took off the pin and tied on a cork instead; but he doubts whether that will catch fish as well. He tells me that he is five years old. Indeed I was present at the celebration of his birthday lately, and supplied the company with onion and squash pipes, and rhubarb whistles, which is the most I can do on such occasions. Little Sammy Hoar blew them most successfully, and made the loudest noise, though it almost strained his eyes out to do it. Edith is full of spirits. When she comes home from school she goes hop, skip and jump down into the field to pick berries, currants, gooseberries, raspberries, and thimble-berries. . . .

"I found a nice penknife on the bank of the river this afternoon, which was probably lost by some villager who went there to bathe lately. Yesterday I found a nice arrowhead, which was lost some time before by an Indian who was hunting there. The knife was a very little rusted; the arrowhead was not rusted at all. . . .

"Do not think you must write to me," [he concluded] "because I have written to you. It does not follow at all. You would not naturally make so long a speech to me here in a month as a letter would be. Yet if some time it should be perfectly easy and pleasant to you, I shall be very glad to have a sentence.

"Your old acquaintance,

Henry Thoreau."

He was not tied to the Emerson house. He still took his solitary walks. He worked in his father's pencil factory. He was so skillful at packing the product made by "J. Thoreau & Son" that he could pick up an even dozen with either hand. He had not been content merely to help in the manufacture—he had improved the lead, which was at first gritty, by baking clay with it; but still not satisfied, he invented a process to refine the lead dust. This was a narrow, churnlike chamber around the millstones used to grind the lead, which carried the lead dust seven feet up to a boxlike shelf. Only the finest lead dust rose to the shelf; the rest was ground again. He went further. Instead of casing the lead with two pieces of wood glued together, he designed a machine to drill a round hole in a solid piece of wood.

The drawing teacher of a fashionable school in Boston told her pupils "to ask at the art store for a *Thoreau* pencil, for they are the best."

The factory prospered.

Chapter Ten

In the Public Eye

A LMOST from the time that he had returned from Harvard, Henry Thoreau had made public appearances as a lecturer, first at the Concord Lyceum, where Emerson, Alcott, and others also spoke; afterwards in Salem—at Hawthorne's invitation—in Portland, and Bangor, Maine, and other places. In Concord, he spoke for nothing, but when he went elsewhere he received $20 or $25 for each appearance. Although his lectures—on nature, on literary and civil subjects, on himself—were freighted with great thoughts, greatly expressed, he was not a good public speaker, if by the term is meant one who lets his notes go by the board and holds his audience spellbound. Thoreau seldom looked up from his manuscript. Worse, he alarmed and offended his audiences by telling them what he thought of them.

Some of his lectures, many of his poems, had appeared in print. But like all authors he dreamed of the day when he would have a book to his credit. He had the materials for two.

He had brought back from Walden, besides a refreshed spirit, a huge treasure-trove: his prose journals, from which he had carved out a book entitled *A Week on the Concord and Merrimack Rivers,* whose melancholy publishing history will now be told. He was also to quarry, from the same source, the book that made him famous throughout the world—*Walden, or Life in the Woods.*

Thoreau had read the *Week* to Alcott in his cabin by the pond. Alcott was all enthusiasm. He wrote in his journal:

"The book is purely American, fragrant with the life of New England woods and streams, and could have been written nowhere else. Especially am I touched by his sufficiency and soundness, his aboriginal vigor—as if a man had once more come into Nature who knew what Nature meant him to do with her; Virgil and White of Selborne, and Izaak Walton, and Yankee settler all in one. I came home at midnight through the snowy woodpaths, and slept with the pleasing dream that presently the press would give me two books to be proud of—Emerson's *Poems* and Thoreau's *Week.*"

Emerson, after hearing some of the *Week* read, wrote to a friend: "In a short time, if Wiley and Putnam smile, you shall have Henry Thoreau's *Excursion on the Concord and Merrimack Rivers,* a seven days' voyage in as many chapters, pastoral as Izaak Walton, spicy as flagroot. . . . He read me some of it under an oak on the river bank the other afternoon and invigorated me."

Wiley and Putnam were New York publishers. They did not smile. Neither did Thoreau when he received the manuscript back. By the end of the year four publishers had rejected it. Encouraged by Emerson, he decided to print the book at his own expense, and signed a contract with the Boston firm of James Munroe. The book was finally published in May, 1849, and Thoreau's hopes were high. Into it he had put not only the exciting account of the river voyage with his brother John, previously related, but an anthology of his reading in literature and philosophy. To no avail. Though James Russell Lowell praised the author in the *Massachusetts Quarterly Review* as "both wise man and poet," the book fell stillborn from the press, and Thoreau was out of pocket. In addition, his publisher, "falsely so called," as Thoreau noted in his journal, hounded him about the disposition of the unsold copies—706, out of an edition of 1,000. Munroe had written that 'he had use for the room they occupied in his cellar." Thoreau sent for them.

The unsold books gave him the opportunity to pen what was to become a famous remark in the annals of authorship: "I have now a library of nearly nine hundred volumes, over seven hundred of which I wrote myself." He found that "they are something more substantial than fame, as my back knows, which has borne them up two flights of stairs." His sense of humor persisted:

"There was just one piece of good luck in the venture. The unbound copies were tied up by the printer four years ago in stout paper wrappers, and inscribed—

'H. D. Thoreau's
Concord River
50 cops.'

So Munroe had only to cross out 'River,' and write 'Mass.' and deliver them to the expressman."

Having stacked the copies, he turned once more to his journal: "Nevertheless, in spite of this result, sitting beside the inert mass of my works, I take up my pen tonight to record what thought or experience I may have had, with as much satisfaction as ever. Indeed, I believe that this result is more inspiring and better for me than if a thousand had bought my wares. It affects my privacy less and leaves me freer."

It was a disappointment, all the same. It rankled. It rankled even more when he had to work overtime manufacturing thousands of pencils, which he sold below cost, to raise the money with which to pay off Munroe.

He felt the need of fresh air. On October 9, 1849, he left Concord for Boston, bound for a walking tour of Cape Cod.

A handbill announced the wreck of a Galway brig: "Death!" it screamed. "One hundred and forty-five lives lost at Cohasset." Thoreau decided to go by way of Cohasset.

The melancholy labors on the beach were still under way, two days after the wreck. The two-masted square-rigged vessel, crowded with emigrants, had been dashed on the rocks, on which the sea was still breaking violently. In a rocky cove he saw part of one side of the vessel, about forty feet long and fourteen wide:

"The largest timbers and iron braces were broken superfluously, and I saw that no material could withstand the power of the waves; that iron must go to pieces in such a case, and an iron vessel would be cracked up like an egg-shell on the rocks."

"This is said to be the rockiest shore in Massachusetts, from Nantasket to Scituate," he noted.

Did he think of Ellen Sewall when he wrote these words? His own life had been shipwrecked once by the siren of Scituate.

His description of Cape Cod, to which the Pilgrims had first come, is justly famous:

"Cape Cod is the bared and bended arm of Massachusetts: the shoulder is at Buzzard's Bay; the elbow, or crazy-bone, at Cape Mallebarre; the wrist at Truro; and the sandy fist at Provincetown—behind which the State stands on her guard, with her back to the Green Mountains, and her feet planted on the floor of the ocean, like an athlete protecting her Bay—boxing with northeast storms, and, ever and anon, heaving up her Atlantic adversary from the lap of earth—ready to thrust forward her other fist, which keeps guard the while upon her breast at Cape Ann."

He returned to his bachelor existence in Concord. The Thoreau family had moved from the outskirts of the town to a house on Main Street. In cold weather, his garret room was uninhabitable, and he had to sit downstairs, particularly in the evening, surrounded by his family, an aunt, a boarder or two. There was only one way to get away from them all, and that was to get outdoors. He solved the problem in a practical fashion. He became a surveyor. The instruments he purchased for this occupation can still be seen in the Concord Library. Before he was through, he had become the chief surveyor of the town. He was, as he pronounced his name, "thorough." He took more offsets than any other surveyor. He rectified old boundaries. Sam Staples had just bought some land next to Emerson's, and one day Thoreau called the philosopher from his study and smilingly asked: "Why will you steal your neighbor's meadow?"

He showed Emerson that his hedge and ditch were well inside the Staples property. As for Staples, when Thoreau told him, he replied: "No matter; let the ditch be the line."

A receipted bill in the Middlebury College library indicates Thoreau's work and wages. For "surveying a woodlot in the east part of Concord, making a Plan, and calculating two Areas; also—to laying out a street and House-lots near the middle of the town—& making a plan of the same—seven dollars."

Five years passed. Although he had announced in the *Week* that *Walden* was ready and "will soon be published," his experience with Munroe deterred him from a new venture into publishing. Now he went ahead. This time he had a real publisher, Ticknor and Fields, of Boston, famous in the annals of American literature. There was no payment demanded from the author.

He had already published two extracts from this book in a magazine. Now *The Tribune,* of New York, in advance of publication, printed three and a third columns of small type from it, creating more interest in the book than a review could have done. Two thousand copies of *Walden* were sold. Later, Ticknor and Fields reissued the earlier volume. Slowly, but surely, Thoreau's fame began to be established. Even locally—for farmers and laborers came to his house in the morning to ask what the weather would be!

Meanwhile, he continued to keep his journals going. He was now a corresponding member of the Boston Society of Natural History. Although his surveying jobs kept him a great deal in the open, bringing new adventures in the realm that he loved, they were not enough, and he continued to take walks of his own, free to observe Nature. He folded back the lining of his hat, to make a receptacle for flowers and rare plants encountered on his walks; and sometimes carried an old music book for pressing them. And now, able to afford it at last, he bought a spyglass for bird watching. Nothing escaped his vigilant gaze—only he could have written, after one of his walks: "I had no idea that there was so much going on in Heywood's meadow."

His old habitation still lured him:

"Walked to Walden last night (moon not quite full). . . .

"As I climbed the hill again toward my old bean-field, I listened to the ancient, familiar, immortal, dear cricket sound under all others, hearing at first some distinct chirps; but when these ceased I was aware of the general earth-song, which my hearing had not heard, amid which these were only taller flowers in a bed, and I wondered if behind or beneath this there was not some other chant yet more universal."

Chapter Eleven

Thoreau Meets Walt Whitman

IT WAS his friend Alcott who led Thoreau into the biggest surveying job of his career. But it was not in Concord. The place was Eagleswood, an establishment for "radical opinions and old-fashioned culture," together with a school for the young, near Perth Amboy, New Jersey. It was also a gathering place for Abolitionists. A former Presidential candidate was there—J. G. Birney, of Alabama, who had freed his slaves to run on an anti-slavery ticket in 1844. The school itself was conducted by Theodore Weld, an anti-slavery orator and director of Abolitionist groups throughout the country. Horace Greeley, the powerful editor of the New York *Tribune,* was a visitor. Alcott was there, holding "conversations," on which he doted. He wrote to Thoreau to come, to survey the establishment's two hundred acres, lay out streets, and give lectures as occasion served.

Thoreau did not like group enterprises of any description. Still, it was tempting. He went. He stayed nearly all of November, 1856. He worked hard. He wrote to his sister Sophia:

"This is a queer place . . . .

"I said just enough to set them a little by the ears and make it lively. I had excused myself by saying that I could not adapt myself to a particular audience; for all the speaking and lecturing here have reference to the children, who are far the greater part of the audience, and they are not so bright as New England children. Imagine them sitting close to the wall, all around a hall, with old Quaker-looking men and women here and there."

There were a lot of long white beards, on which he remarked, and one elderly gray-headed lady "in extreme Bloomer costume, which was what you may call remarkable." He described one of the men, who had a "broad face and a great white beard, looking like a pier-head made of the cork-tree with the bark on, as if he could buffet a considerable wave."

"Some of them, I suspect, are very worthy people," he added.

He was glad, however, to get away from them:

"I have been constantly engaged in surveying Eagleswood—through woods, salt marshes, and along the shore, dodging the tide, through bushes, mud, and beggar-ticks, having no time to look up or think where I am. (It takes ten or fifteen minutes before each meal to pick the beggar-ticks out of my clothes; burrs and the rest are left, and rents mended at the first convenient opportunity.)"

But there were always meals to return to, and the inevitable gatherings: "The hardest thing to find here is solitude—and Concord."

He was glad to go off on side excursions to New York with his friend Alcott, who knew everybody. They heard Henry Ward Beecher preach. They went to literary socials. They spent a day at Horace Greeley's farm at Chappaqua, in Westchester County. And they went to call on Walt Whitman.

Only a year before, Whitman, the poet of Democracy, had published *Leaves of Grass,* which he had sent to Emerson. Emerson recognized its worth. "I greet you at the beginning of a great career," he had written to the then unknown Brooklyn poet. Whitman printed these words across the back of the next edition.

Emerson's words were prophetic—the book brought a new greatness to the land, though some were slow to see that its author had ushered in, not only a great new personality and genius, but the "years of the modern," as Whitman himself phrased it.

Thoreau was two years older than Whitman—thirty-nine to the latter's thirty-seven. Walt's dress was even more unconventional than Henry's. He received people in his attic study in a striped calico jacket, with a red flannel undershirt open at the neck, and overalls. Thus Alcott has described his attire. In his journal he wrote:

"I hoped to put him into communication direct with Thoreau, and tried my hand a little after we came down stairs and sat in the parlor below; but each seemed planted fast in reserves, surveying the other curiously—like two beasts, each wondering what the other would do, whether to snap or run; and it came to no more than cold compliments between them."

Such was the meeting between the author of *Walden* and the poet of *Leaves of Grass*. But Whitman had made a profound impression on Thoreau, as it turned out; for Henry wrote:

"He is apparently the greatest democrat the world has seen. Kings and aristocracy go by the board at once, as they have long deserved to. A remarkably strong though coarse nature, of a sweet disposition, and much prized by his friends . . . .

"He told us that he loved to ride up and down Broadway all day on an omnibus, sitting beside the driver, listening to the roar of the carts, and sometimes ges-

ticulating and declaiming Homer at the top of his
voice. . . ."

Again: "I have just read his second edition (which
he gave me), and it has done me more good than any
reading for a long time."

How did Thoreau impress Whitman? The poet's
biographer has recorded Walt's recollections of their
meeting:

"Thoreau's great fault was disdain—disdain for
men (for Tom, Dick, and Harry): inability to appre-
ciate the average life—even the exceptional life: it
seemed to me a want of imagination. He couldn't put
his life into any other life—realize why one man was
so and another man was not so: was impatient with
other people on the street and so forth. We had a hot
discussion about it—it was a bitter difference: it was
rather a surprise to me to meet in Thoreau such a very
aggravated case of superciliousness. It was egotistic
—not taking that word in its worst sense."

Someone who was present when Whitman was char-
acterizing Thoreau in this manner remarked that the
latter was "simply selfish—that's the long and short
of it."

Said Whitman: "That may be the short of it but it's
not the long. Selfish? No—not selfish in the way you

mean, though selfish, sure enough, in a higher inter-
pretation of that term. We could not agree at all in our
estimate of men—of the men we meet here, there,
everywhere—the concrete man. Thoreau had an abstraction about man—a right abstraction: there we
agreed. We had our quarrel only on this ground. Yet
he was a man you would have to like—an interesting
man, simple, conclusive."

Thoreau was glad to get back to Concord. But now
his walks and meditations were profoundly disturbed.

Chapter Twelve

The Speech in the Vestry

O N JULY 4, 1854, Thoreau had delivered an address, entitled "Slavery in Massachusetts," before the Anti-Slavery Convention at Framingham. It was printed in the *Liberator*, organ of the Abolitionists, two weeks later. It was a stirring attack on the Fugitive Slave Law of 1850, whose inhumanity and viciousness had been brought home to the people of New England by the seizure and trial of an escaped slave, Anthony Burns, in Boston.

Said Thoreau at Framingham: "I lately attended a meeting of the citizens of Concord, expecting, as one among many, to speak on the subject of slavery in Massachusetts; but I was surprised and disappointed to find that what had called my townsmen together was the destiny of Nebraska, and not of Massachusetts, and that what I had to say would be entirely out of order. I had thought that the house was on fire, and not the prairie; but though several of the citizens of Massachusetts are now in prison for attempting to rescue a slave from her own clutches, not one of the speakers at that meeting expressed regret for it, not one even referred to it. . . ."

What did it matter to him whether Nebraska came into the Union slave or free? Nebraska was far away, while Massachusetts, his own state, was aiding and abetting the slaveholders of the South. He applied his scorn and indignation locally:

"Again it happens that the Boston Court House is full of armed men, holding prisoner and trying a *man*, to find out if he is not really a *slave*. Does anyone think that justice or God awaits Mr. Loring's decision? For him to sit there deciding still, when this question is already decided from eternity to eternity, and the unlettered slave himself and the multitude around have long since heard and assented to the decision, is simply to make himself ridiculous. . . .

"The whole military force of the State is at the service of a Mr. Suttle, a slaveholder from Virginia, to enable him to catch a man whom he calls his property; but not a soldier is offered to save a citizen of Massachusetts from being kidnapped! . . .

"I wish my countrymen to consider, that whatever the human law may be, neither an individual nor a

nation can ever commit the least act of injustice against
the obscurest individual without having to pay the
penalty of it. A government which deliberately enacts
injustice, and persists in it, will at length even become
the laughing-stock of the world."

He did not appear prepossessing. But the force of
his words *told* what his delivery and appearance lacked.
True to himself, he could not leave Nature out, and
he concluded his address as follows:

"I walk toward one of our ponds; but what signifies
the beauty of Nature when men are base? We walk to
lakes to see our serenity reflected in them; when we
are not serene, we go not to them. Who can be serene
in a country where both the rulers and the ruled are
without principle? The remembrance of my country
spoils my walk."

The incident at Boston Court House had stirred
other writers besides Thoreau to indignation and pro-
test. John Greenleaf Whittier wrote, in his poem "The
Rendition," about the seizure of Anthony Burns:

And, as I thought of Liberty
    Marched handcuffed down that sworded street,
    The solid earth beneath my feet
Reeled fluid as the sea.

In New York, Walt Whitman wrote "A Boston Ballad." He saw clearly that tyranny had returned in a new guise:

> How bright shine the cutlasses of the foremost troops!
> Every man holds his revolver, marching stiff through Boston town.

He suggested that the Mayor "send a committee to England"—

> They shall get a grant from the Parliament, to go with a cart to the royal vault,
> Dig out King George's coffin . . . .

Five years after Thoreau spoke at Framingham, the issue that was slowly but surely tearing the Union apart hung like an ominous cloud over the young Republic. Now it was 1859. He had given—and was to give—to the issue all his passion and strength, like a man who knows he has not long to live, and so pours forth his powers with a prodigal hand.

A climax was near. John Brown, soliciting funds in New England, came to Concord. It was his second appearance there. Two years before, on a previous visit

of the famous anti-slavery fighter, Thoreau had sub-
scribed "a trifle" to help keep Kansas free.

"I had so much confidence in the man—that he
would do right," Thoreau wrote in his journal; "but
it would seem that he had not confidence enough in
me, nor in anybody else that I know, to communicate
his plans to us."

Brown was as impressive as before when he spoke
at the Concord Town Hall. He had a spare figure,
patriarchal beard and flashing eyes, and an aura of
action and invincibility about him. Had he not rescued
slaves, and with a handful of men escorted them
through slave territory to Canada and freedom? But
he was not more communicative now than he had been
previously. Conservative Concord would have been
surprised—perhaps horrified—to know what he had
in mind: the establishment of a strong point from which
to make sporadic raids to free slaves.

On June 30, 1859, Brown arrived at Harper's Ferry,
Virginia (now West Virginia), thirty miles south of
the Pennsylvania border. There was a United States
arsenal at Harper's Ferry. He leased a farm, and
spent the next ten weeks collecting twenty-one followers
and arms, which they carted from Chambersburg,
Pennsylvania. Then, on October, 16, with eighteen of
his followers, he seized the arsenal by direct assault.
Virginia sent a detachment of militia to besiege him,

and he was able to hold out only twenty-four hours. The militia was commanded by Colonel Robert E. Lee and Lieutenant J. E. B. Stuart. Ten of Brown's followers were killed in the fighting, seven escaped, and Brown and four of his men were taken prisoner. After a trial, he was sentenced to be hanged. The news of his spectacular thrust against the slave-power, and of his sentence, had reached and rocked the North.

On October 30, while Brown lay under sentence of death, Thoreau, who had been writing feverishly for several days, sent a boy around Concord to notify his fellow townsmen that he would speak in the vestry of the church in defense of Captain John Brown. One of them sent back word that he "thought it a bad thing to do, that the time was dangerous, and it would be better to wait until there was a better feeling among the people."

Thoreau sent the boy back.

"Tell Mr. Sanborn," he told the boy to say, "that he has misunderstood the announcement, that there is to be a meeting in the vestry, and that Mr. Thoreau will speak."

To a solemn, and in part an unfriendly audience, Thoreau delivered one of the great American orations. Emerson was there, and noted that the speech "was heard by all respectfully, by many with a sympathy that surprised themselves."

Said Thoreau: "If this man's acts and words do not create a revival, it will be the severest possible satire on the acts and words that do. It is the best news that America has ever heard. It has already quickened the feeble pulse of the North, and infused more and more generous blood into her veins and heart than any number of years of what is called commercial and political prosperity could. How many a man who was lately contemplating suicide has now something to live for! . . .

"Think of him—of his rare qualities!—such a man as it takes ages to make, and ages to understand; no mock hero, nor the representative of any party. A man such as the sun may not rise upon again in this be-nighted land. To whose making went the costliest material, the finest adamant; sent to be the redeemer of those in captivity; and the only use to which you can put him is to hang him at the end of a rope!"

He quoted Brown himself as he stood trial: " 'I pity the poor in bondage that have none to help them; that is why I am here; not to gratify any personal animosity, revenge, or vindictive spirit. It is my sympathy with the oppressed and the wronged, that are as good as you, and as precious in the sight of God.' "

Said Thoreau: "You don't know your testament when you see it." He continued to quote Brown: " 'I want you to understand that I respect the rights of the poorest and weakest of colored people, oppressed by the slave power, just as much as I do those of the most wealthy and powerful.' "

He repeated Brown's prophetic words: " 'I wish to say, furthermore, that you had better, all you people at the South, prepare yourselves for a settlement of that question, that must come up for settlement sooner than you are prepared for it. The sooner you are prepared the better. You may dispose of me very easily. I am nearly disposed of now [he had been severely wounded in the fighting at Harper's Ferry]; but this question is still to be settled—this Negro question, I mean; the end of that is not yet.' "

Said Thoreau: "I foresee the time when the painter will paint that scene, no longer going to Rome for a subject; the poet will sing it; the historian record it; and, with the Landing of the Pilgrims and the Declaration of Independence, it will be the ornament of some future national gallery, when at least the present form of slavery shall be no more here. We shall then be at liberty to weep for Captain Brown."

Thoreau read his speech again, first in Worcester, then to an immense audience in Boston Temple. Perhaps he was conscious of historic forces at work, himself a part. Brown was hanged on December 2. Because it was thought an attempt might be made to rescue him, fifteen hundred soldiers formed a hollow square around the scaffold.

Two years later, Union troops were marching to the tune and the words of "John Brown's Body."

Chapter Thirteen

The Death of Thoreau

THOREAU was not well, although it was at first
not apparent. He was still walking, still keeping the
great mass of his journal going. "Each town," he
wrote, "should have a park, or rather a primitive forest,
of five hundred or a thousand acres, where a stick
should never be cut for fuel, a common possession forever, for instruction and recreation. We hear of cow-
commons and ministerial lots, but we want *men*-com-
mons and lay lots, inalienable forever. Let us keep the
New World *new*, preserve all the advantages of living
in the country."

Meanwhile, *his* park was the woods. On December
3, 1860, at Smith's Hill, near the Cambridge Turnpike, he counted the rings on a hickory that had been
cut down. It was a raw day, presaging snow. He came
home with a severe cold, which developed into bron-
chitis.

The spring of 1861 was the spring of Civil War; the issue of slavery had been joined at last, and Thoreau found in the response of the North to the firing on Fort Sumter a sense of an America regenerated. He told his sister Sophia that he would never get well until the war was over, and for a man who had recorded his dislike of newspapers, he read the war news avidly.

It was thought that a sojourn in a dry climate might benefit his lungs. In May he set out for Minnesota. He was gone two months. As his train approached Minneapolis, he saw, from the window, a wild crabapple tree in bloom. Weak as he was, he later sought and found the tree. It was his last "appointment" with Nature. He returned as ill as he had left. His narrow rattan daybed, which he had made himself, was brought down from his upstairs study. At mealtimes he left his bed to sit with his family at table. But soon he was unable to do even this much. His voice dwindled to a whisper.

Visitors came. Boys brought him game and flowers from the woods that he loved. The older people, with deeper concerns, talked to him of his soul. He was not very patient.

Parker Pillsbury, a friend of the family, tried to talk to him about the next world.

"One world at a time," Thoreau whispered.

His Aunt Louisa asked him if he had made his peace with God.

"I did not know we had quarreled," he replied.

Sam Staples, the genial jailor, came to see him, and reported to Emerson: "Never spent an hour with more satisfaction. Never saw a man dying with so much pleasure and peace."

As he sank into the shadows, Thoreau whispered: "Moose . . . Indians." At length, at nine in the morning, May 6, 1862, while sitting up on his couch, he died, apparently without pain. He was buried in Concord's Sleepy Hollow Cemetery, and over his grave was placed a small stone with a single word chiseled on it:

"HENRY."

Chapter Fourteen

Epilogue

CONCORD had given him a public funeral—a last irony for this private-souled man. In the hushed parish church, Bronson Alcott read one of Thoreau's poems, and Ralph Waldo Emerson, with a faltering voice, delivered a eulogy of his dead friend.

"He chose, wisely, no doubt, for himself," Emerson said, "to be a bachelor of thought and Nature. He had no talent for wealth, and knew how to be poor without the least hint of squalor or inelegance. Perhaps he fell into his way of living without forecasting it much, but approved it with later wisdom. 'I am often reminded,' he wrote in his journal, 'that, if I had bestowed on me the wealth of Croesus, my aims must be still the same, and my means essentially the same.' He had no temptations to fight against—no appetites, no passions, no taste for elegant trifles. A fine house, dress, the manners and talk of highly cultivated people were all thrown away on him. He much preferred a good Indian, and considered these refinements as impediments to conversation, wishing to meet his companion on the simplest terms . . . .

"He chose to be rich **by making his wants few, and** supplying them himself. In his travels, he used the railroad only to get over so much country as was unimportant to the present purpose, walking hundreds of miles, avoiding taverns, buying a lodging in farmers' and fishermens' houses, as cheaper, and more agreeable to him, and because there he could better find the men and the information he wanted . . . .

"Yet, hermit and stoic as he was, he was really fond of sympathy, and threw himself heartily and childlike into the company of young people whom he loved, and whom he delighted to entertain, as he only could, with the varied and endless anecdotes of his experiences by field and river; and he was always ready to lead a huckleberry party or a search for chestnuts or grapes . . . .

"No truer American existed than Thoreau. His preference of his country and condition was genuine, and his aversation from English and European manners and tastes almost reached contempt. He listened impatiently to news or *bons mots* gleaned from London circles; and though he tried to be civil, these anecdotes fatigued him. The men were all imitating each other,

and on a small mold. Why can they not live as far apart as possible, and each be a man by himself? What he sought was the most energetic Nature; and he wished to go to Oregon, not to London . . . .

"His robust common sense, armed with stout hands, keen perceptions, and strong will, cannot yet account for the superiority which shone in his simple and hidden life. I must add the cardinal fact, that there was an excellent wisdom in him, proper to a rare class of men, which showed him the material world as a means and symbol . . . .

"He understood the matter in hand at a glance, and saw the limitations and poverty of those he talked with, so that nothing seemed concealed from such terrible eyes. I have repeatedly known young men of sensibility converted in a moment to the belief that this was the man they were in search of, the man of men, who could tell them all they should do. His own dealing with them was never affectionate, but superior, didactic, scorning their petty ways—very slowly conceding, or not conceding at all, the promise of his society at their houses, or even at his own. 'Would he not walk with them?' 'He did not know. There was nothing so important to him as his walk; he had no walks to throw away on company' . . . .

"Mr. Thoreau dedicated his genius with such entire love to the fields, hills, and waters of his native town that he made them known and interesting to all reading Americans, and to people over the sea . . . .

"It was a pleasure and a privilege to walk with him. He knew the country like a fox or a bird, and passed through it as freely by paths of his own. He knew every track in the snow or on the ground, and what creature had taken this path before him. One must submit abjectly to such a guide, and the reward was great . . . .

"The country knows not yet, or in the least part, how great a son it has lost. It seems an injury that he should leave in the midst his broken task which none else can finish, a kind of indignity to so noble a soul that he should depart out of Nature before yet he has been really shown to his peers for what he is. But he, at least, is content. His soul was made for the noblest society; he had in a short life exhausted the capabilities of this world; wherever there is knowledge, wherever there is virtue, wherever there is beauty, he will find a home."